# Letters
## to
# College Presidents

*Every man who knows how to read has it in his power to magnify himself, to multiply the ways in which he exists, to make his life full, significant, and interesting.*

—ALDOUS HUXLEY

# Letters

## to

# College Presidents

Thomas E. Jones

Edward V. Stanford, O.S.A.

Goodrich C. White

*Englewood Cliffs, N. J.*
PRENTICE-HALL, INC.

378
J12 L

48,323
Dec. 1964

# Foreword

The genesis of the Administrative Consultant Service of the Association of American Colleges was an informal chat between Dr. Harold Duling of Lilly Endowment, Inc., and myself as we were strolling around on the grounds in Pugwash, Nova Scotia, at the first Intellectual Life Conference of the Association. We both expressed concern about the most harried man in America, the college president. We felt that it would be helpful if college presidents could consult with experienced retired presidents in a purely personal and informal way. This idea was enthusiastically accepted by the Board of Directors of the Association and financially supported by Lilly Endowment, Inc.

The program was begun in 1958 with Dr. Thomas E. Jones, retired president of Earlham College, and Dr. Goodrich C. White, retired president of Emory University, as the first two consultants. In 1960 Father Edward V. Stanford, former president of Villanova University, was added to the team of consultants. These three men, at the invitation of the presidents, visited over 250 institutions for periods of from two to five days and engaged in discussions with presidents, trustees, faculty and students on a wide variety of problems confronting the presidents. When the program had been in successful operation for some four years, it occurred to the writer of this foreword that it might be helpful to a still larger audience of presidents, trustees, faculty members and others concerned with the welfare of our colleges if the experience accumulated by the three consultants would be distilled into a series of informal letters to college presidents.

On behalf of the Association of American Colleges, I hereby record the deepest appreciation of the Association to the consultants themselves and to Lilly Endowment, without whose interest and support neither this book nor the still continuing program would have been possible.

THEODORE A. DISTLER

5

# Introduction

These "letters" are an outgrowth of the Administrative Consultant Service of the Association of American Colleges. They deal informally with some of the administrative problems which the three consultants met on their visits to almost 300 colleges and universities. The "letter" format was adopted the better to capture this informality and to avoid pretentiousness.

It need hardly be said that the book does not pretend to be a comprehensive treatise on college administration or the presidential office. Nor do the letters constitute official recommendations from the Association of American Colleges. It would be highly presumptuous to suggest that anyone could draft a completely reliable guide to success as a college president, provide formulae covering every detail of college administration, or write prescriptions for the cure of every administrative disorder. It was believed, however, that it might be helpful to put before member presidents some of the reflections and advice that emerged from the actual experience of the consultants.

No attempt has been made systematically to develop or expound an educational philosophy, though certainly, at least by implication, certain guiding principles, predilections, even prejudices, are manifest. Where these appear, as also in the case of specific practical proposals, the intention of the authors has been to avoid dogmatic pronouncements and to offer suggestions only.

All three of the consultants have had a hand in the preparation of each of the letters. As nearly as possible, consensus has been achieved. Nevertheless, no one of the three should be supposed to subscribe to every idea expressed or to every suggestion advanced.

In the main the letters are to be thought of as addressed to the presidents of relatively small colleges, chiefly independent or "church-related" and chiefly concerned in emphasizing the liberal arts. Most of the colleges visited by the consultants were of this type, though some larger, more complex institutions and some tax-supported institutions were included in the visits which the consultants were invited to make.

The letters are addressed to fictitious presidents of imaginary colleges. They do not, however, deal with fictitious or imaginary problems. On each problem discussed college presidents have actually sought advice from one or other of the three consultants. None of the letters deals with an issue or a situation precisely like that encountered at a particular college. But the situations and the problems are real.

While much of the discussion may seem to the experienced educator quite elementary, it must be remembered that in at least a number of instances the letters are addressed to "new" presidents who come to this highly critical area of educational administration with no previous experience. Beyond this, there are positive suggestions and cautions which may be of value even to the veteran president who encounters problems that are new to him.

The authors wish to record their gratitude to colleagues who have been most directly related to the consultant program and to the subsequent production of these letters. Dr. Theodore A. Distler provided leadership, guidance and encouragement throughout. Mr. Harold Duling's faith in the proposal assured its financing by Lilly Endowment, Inc. His associate, Dr. Manning Pattillo, from the beginning took a helpful interest in the work of the consultants and contributed importantly to the determination of the format and the content of the letters. In the preparation of the final text the editorial *expertise* of Mr. F. L. Wormald was invaluable in smoothing out roughnesses of style and in securing consensus when inconsistencies or disagreements appeared.

Gratitude is recorded also to the officers of the Association of American Colleges for their sponsorship of the program and for their generous expressions of approval of the work of the consultants. Finally, our thanks go to the hundreds of college presidents, deans, other administrative officers, and faculty members who received the visiting consultants graciously and engaged with them in the sharing of ideas and the facing of problems of mutual interest and concern.

Participation in the consultant service has been for the three of us an interesting and rewarding experience. Whatever contribution it may have made to the work of the colleges, we ourselves have been furnished with new insights, strengthened faith in the future of higher education, and a heightened admiration for the men and women whose lives are devoted to the service of our colleges and thus to the young people upon whom will rest responsibility for America's tomorrows.

THOMAS E. JONES
EDWARD V. STANFORD, O.S.A.
GOODRICH C. WHITE

# Contents

9

# 1

## The Presidential Predicament

First, allow me to congratulate you on a very impressive inauguration. The whole affair was brilliantly planned and executed. Under your leadership one can expect great things.

I am particularly interested, and somewhat amused, by one question you asked me: "Why has this appointment made such a difference in the attitude of my friends and of people in the community?" You say that faculty members and administrative colleagues who only a short time ago would drop in informally for a cup of tea now pass by or wait for an invitation; and others who used to treat you as an ordinary citizen are now too formal or overanxious to please.

I am not surprised. I have had similar experiences, and now I am finding that my role as a consultant seems different in the eyes of my friends. In my travels I have found other presidents bothered by this same experience. It is not easy to go through; sometimes one wonders whether something is wrong with oneself or with one's friends. Wasn't it a veteran college president who said to a recent appointee: "Young man, you have changed your profession. Watch out, or it will change you!" On reflection, I think you will see that these reactions are normal.

The authority and prestige that go with the office of president alter a man's status. He has to repeat, at least annually before a commencement audience: *"By the authority vested in me . . ."* The public identifies a president with the institution he represents and judges him accordingly. The members of the college family depend on the institution and on the president for their security and advancement. In view of these attitudes and relationships, I think you will agree that the reactions you are experiencing are natural. The important thing is not to let them upset you or make you oversensitive toward those with whom you have to work.

I have known presidents who have become so self-conscious that they have widened rather than closed the normal gap that exists between them and their associates. On the other hand, there are those who have tried to be so chummy that they have lost the respect of their colleagues. To strike a balance is not easy. The only way I know is to be your real self and to recognize that, as one's profession changes, one's relationship to others is changed correspondingly.

In order to maintain proper man-to-man relationships, I have found some presidents arranging informal evenings with individuals and faculty groups. At such gatherings any subject outside of college or university matters may be discussed. Sometimes refreshments are served, sometimes not. Often the meetings are held in the president's home, but they may convene in the faculty club or at a downtown hotel, in which case they may be followed by a concert or some other function. In one university I found a president holding meetings each week with ten or a dozen heads of departments, instructors and administrative assistants. These groups rotated so as to permit every member of the faculty and staff to have at least one session with the president. The informal conversations at such meetings have proved to be an effective means of enabling administrators and teachers to get to know each other and to work together more effectively.

Similar informal gatherings have also proved useful in getting to know students and gaining their support in the larger issues of college policy. In some cases students have abused this friendly give-and-take and have become overfamiliar. It is said that, before the first name habit of the present generation became so pronounced, an unsophisticated freshman addressed

Vanderbilt University's kindly but dignified President James H. Kirkland with "Good morning, Prexy." Kirkland called the youth over and said, "Look here, young man, if you want to be familiar with me, you might like to know that my friends call me Jimmy." Needless to say, the student never made that mistake again.

It is not easy, as I have said, to find a balance between the formal and informal requirements of a president's office. Individuals must somehow sense this balance and, with friendliness and courage, go on being themselves.

After all, perhaps this relationship rests upon the nature of the college and the community in which it is located. As a chief executive meets his responsibilities, his relationships with his associates naturally take on new dimensions. There is no doubt that the requirements for the president of a college or university are high and that those who occupy the office are bound accordingly. I once saw a statement of such requirements which astonished me. One needed to be a scholar, an educator, a financier, an orator, a diplomat, a family man and a spiritual leader. To measure up to such requirements, one president said that a man had to have the "courage of a David, the wisdom of a Solomon, the zeal of a St. Paul and the patience of a Job."

Undoubtedly, scholarship, imagination, physical vigor, ability to speak, integrity and managerial skill are important; and trustees and public relations officers like to point out these qualities. Be that as it may, presidents must never forget that *it is the office, not the president, that is important.* If all eyes can be focused upon the office and the institution it represents, most of the problems I have mentioned will disappear. It is gratifying to note that, as one visits the homes of America's college administrators, one finds that they are a fine lot, and generally measure up to the exacting standards set for them. As scholar, manager, public figure and head of a family, the president helps his college to grow, and the college, in turn, makes the president an educational statesman.

Doubtless this letter contains very little that you do not already know. I am confident that you and your charming wife have long since found the answer to your question, and I am sure that your associates will do likewise.

It was a joy being in your home, and I hope you will stop by to see us whenever you are in this locality.

Sincerely,

# 2

## *The President and the Trustees*

Dear President Armitage:

I am sorry that this letter has been unavoidably delayed. You may be sure that it is the pressure of other demands on my time and not lack of interest that accounts for the delay. I am glad to have your reminder of my agreement to write you, for your perusal alone, a letter about the problem we discussed at some length. That particular problem precipitated the whole question of your relationships with the members of your board of trustees.

You are able to tell me now that the issue has been resolved in reasonably satisfactory fashion, but only after some uncertainty as to the outcome. I got the impression in our conversation that the issue arose unexpectedly and almost as a shock to you. You found yourself confronted by a really serious threat to your own and to institutional integrity. It became clear that you would have to take a firm stand against an influential member of your board. This was not easy for you. Your personal relationship to this trustee had been most cordial. In some ways he had been quite helpful. But, once you had made the issue clear, other members of the board came to your support and the decision was as you wished. I am glad that you stuck it out—even fought it out—and that you did not resign, as at one time you thought you might have to.

It now seems very likely that this unpleasant episode may be productive of some real good for you and for the college. Certainly it must have led to serious reappraisal on the part of board members of their responsibilities and of their relationships to you as president of the college.

In recent years there has been much discussion of the functions and authority of boards of trustees. Articles in the educational journals and a few books are available. There have also been meetings at which trustees of different institutions were brought together for discussion of their duties and their problems. With careful winnowing, such writing and discussion can be helpful. The application of such principles as may emerge becomes the responsibility of the trustees and the president of each individual institution. But the official functions and responsibilities of a board of trustees are one thing: your personal relationships with the members of the board are quite another. It is the latter I'd like to comment on now.

You have a fairly large board, made up of men and women of varied ages, backgrounds, interests and capacities. You want, I am sure, to know each of them as a person and to maintain friendly social relations with them without overdoing it. Some you find more congenial than others. Some you see informally more often than others. Friendly personal contact with members of the board can bring much satisfaction to you and to them. Beyond this is the obvious fact that the better you know and understand the board members the more effectively you can secure their cooperation in the interest of the college.

I am sure that you, like every other college president, have reason to be grateful, for and to, those of your trustees who are consistently understanding, helpful and encouraging. But no president should expect unanimous and automatic approval of all his proposals. There is often need for informal consultation and explanation *before* an important proposal is presented to the board for formal action. A board may be reluctant to act adversely on any recommendation of the president, but its approval should be based on adequate information and understanding. In the course of informal preliminary discussion the president should welcome questions, criticisms and suggestions. You may recall President Wriston's advice: "Proposals ought to be advanced with a view of obtaining consensus. They should be reshaped or modified until a consensus is in sight, or abandoned if compromise has ruined their substance."

All of us owe a great debt to the men and women who give unselfishly of their time, their wisdom and their means in service to our colleges. Whatever the nature of the sponsorship or control of the particular college, theirs is a public trust which involves heavy responsibility. The best of them are devotedly conscientious in recognizing and discharging that responsibility.

But I'd like now to suggest certain types of trustees who, sometimes with the best of intentions, may present problems to the college president. Some of these types I suspect that you have. Certainly the trustee with whom you recently had difficulty falls into one of these categories.

There is almost certain to be an occasional trustee who feels "left out." He thinks he is being ignored, is merely a figurehead, and he resents it. He may or may not be highly successful in his business or profession. In any case he does not like being without recognition or influence as a trustee. You may not be aware of this attitude on his part. But once you discover such a trustee on your board, your course is clear. Call on him for service, use him, put him to work. Otherwise you will lose him.

Of course on any board as large as yours one is apt to find a few members who are perfectly content to be figureheads. In some cases they seldom have anything to say and never volunteer their services. There are even trustees who rarely attend meetings and who seem content merely to have their names printed in the college bulletins. They value, perhaps, the honor of membership but they assume no real responsibility.

Quite in contrast to these first two types is the devoted, deeply interested but overzealous trustee who, without really meaning to, becomes intrusive and meddlesome. He is often an alumnus, and his relationship to the college may long antedate that of the president. He knows its history, he has worked for it, perhaps he has contributed generously to its support. He has come to feel almost as if he "owns" the college. He knows faculty members and their families. He keeps up with "what's going on." He is on the campus frequently. He is popular.

If you have trustees like this, you will need all the tact and skill you can command to reach some understanding with them as to the line between informed and helpful interest on the one hand and meddlesome interference on the other. You want your trustees to visit the campus, of course. You want them to know the faculty. But you do not want them to develop unofficial channels of communication that sometimes provide not information but misinformation, or biased, distorted, misinterpreted information. There is a delicate balance to be maintained here. Awareness of the need for it on the part of trustees and faculty as well as the president is most desirable.

If you have any reason to suspect potential trouble of the kind I am suggesting, try to head it off—but *not* by fiat or regulation. Give your trustees one or two of the published discussions of trusteeship, or get them to attend one or two of the meetings at which trusteeship is discussed. In case of clear and flagrant violations of propriety by a faculty member, you will have to deal directly and firmly with him.

Occasionally one encounters a trustee who can only be described as arrogant. He seems concerned to demonstrate his own superior "executive" ability. He speaks on any issue with dogmatic assurance. He is apt to come up with some proposal for immediate action, which obviously has not been thought through and which runs counter to the plans of the president, who has had no opportunity to consider it. On such an occasion all you can do is play for time. In general you can't do much on your own about such a trustee. He is too sure of himself, and probably not able or willing to listen to anyone else, especially not to a professor, as he is apt to consider the president. You'll have to rely on some other board members who can see this man for what he is and find ways to put a tight rein on him.

In a church-related college one may also find a type of trustee whose main concern seems to be keeping the college "close to the church," or who is always on the alert for some deviation from "the faith," which means his own particular interpretation of creed or doctrine. Be patient with him—but don't let him run over you or stir up too much trouble in the faculty, among the public or in the church press. If you can't control him by gentle but firm persuasion, find a way to get rid of him. I hardly need to say that loyal churchmen, whether ministerial or lay, are not all, or even usually, of this kind. Many of them are understanding, wise and exceedingly helpful.

A different type of watchdog attitude may be displayed by an occasional trustee who is constantly on the alert for any manifestation of economic or social radicalism. He may or may not be identified with any extreme rightist organization. He may well be quite sincere in his conservatism and honestly fearful of anything that seems to him pinkish or leftist. It *may* be possible to reason with him. But if not—if he resorts to direct personal attack on faculty members or to attempts at intimidation—you will have to protest and be ready to fight, even though you may not agree with or approve the particular faculty attitudes he is attacking. Involved here, of course, is the whole complex and delicate question of academic freedom. On this question there is an abundance of published discussion available to you. I need not enlarge on the subject in this letter.

Of course, all these types become really objectionable, even dangerous, whenever they try to interfere or dictate *individually*. Authority vests in the board, *not* in individual board members. Private conference with the president may sometimes be in order if its purpose is to get information and understanding. Insistent demands by an individual trustee for this or that action are *never* in order, and no president should tolerate them. I remember an occasion reported to me by a president whom I knew well. An influential trustee quite rudely and crudely assailed the director of admissions because of his refusal to admit a young relative of the trustee, and then demanded that the president overrule the decision. The president not only promptly refused to accede but made emphatically clear his resentment of this improper approach.

Such action in a specific case is invaluable. It applies policy which may have been vaguely defined but not clearly understood. It reduces the probability of like violations of propriety and protocol. Policy becomes established through practice and is recognized in its applications.

But I do not want to overemphasize difficulties in your relationships with your trustees. Most of your board members,

I am sure, belong in the category of the devotedly conscientious. They present no problem; indeed, you can rely on them for counsel and for support. Though even the best of them may sometimes tax your patience when they do not give approval to your proposals as promptly as you might wish, you can well afford to take all the time and trouble needed to get from them full understanding and genuine commitment to your plans. You are stronger when your policies are theirs too. And such wise and committed members of your board can be helpful when you are occasionally troubled by some of the less admirable types.

I think you have been quite successful in dealing with your trustees, despite your initial tendency to go to individual members too often for advice and help on specific and sometimes quite minor administrative problems. This tendency was probably quite natural when you were a newcomer. It is well that you no longer find it necessary or advisable.

I think too that the recent "run-in," though painful, may have been a proverbial blessing in disguise. It has, I feel sure, cleared the air and strengthened your position as a leader.

Let me hear from you. I am much interested in your plans and your work.

Sincerely,

# 3

## Organizing the Board of Trustees

DEAR PRESIDENT ARMITAGE:

I am happy to have your letter in such prompt reply to mine in which I discussed trustees. I am also greatly pleased that the episode which gave you so much trouble has not only cleared the air but has now led to a definite move on the part of the board of trustees to revise the bylaws, reorganize the committee structure and define procedures more precisely. This, I am sure, is highly gratifying to you.

You are good enough to ask that I work with you and the board's special committee in this process of revision. Certainly I am glad to do so. I shall want to look at *your* board in relationship to the situation and requirements of *your* college. Then, in the light of general principles, I will try to make some specific suggestions for your consideration. Meanwhile I will hold myself in readiness for conference with you at such time as you may suggest, and I shall be glad to see drafts of the proposed new bylaws, or parts of them, as they are developed.

The size and the method of appointment of your board are prescribed in the charter of the college. To make any change in these items would, of course, require legal procedure. I can detect no feeling on your part or on the part of members of your board that such changes would be helpful. I want, however, to make one or two comments on the structure of your board as provided in the charter.

The size of the board seems to me quite satisfactory for your college. It makes possible a good cross section, geographically and occupationally. It also avoids unwieldiness on the one hand and on the other hand too great concentration of power in the hands of a very few—all this, *if* the board is properly organized and *if* it functions effectively.

I note too, and with satisfaction, that: There is provision for alumni representation, carefully safeguarded as to procedures for election by the alumni, with the further requirement that the board itself must approve the alumni choices; there are fairly long terms of office provided for the trustees, with eligibility for re-election but with no life terms; there are no *ex-officio* trustees except the president; and there are no faculty trustees. On this last point there is disagreement in theory and in practice. My own judgment is strongly against faculty representation on the board; I do not spell out my reasons now. My own judgment is also against the president's being a voting member of the board, though here there is much stronger opinion as well as widespread practice to the contrary.

One other comment on the charter provisions for your board. The college is church-related, but your board is, in effect, a self-perpetuating board. There is, of course, the requirement that trustees must be approved, after election, by a designated agency of your church. But no agency of the church *elects* members of the board. And you tell me that in no case has a trustee elected by the board itself been rejected by the church agency.

As a general observation I add this: What church-related means in terms of legal ties, and in terms of intimacy of relationship or directness of control, varies very greatly. You will find instances where there is very great intimacy without any legal or charter provisions for direct control or for election, or even approval, of trustees. In one such case I know of—I am sure there are others—there *is* in the charter a requirement that a specified percentage, a decided majority, of the trustees must belong to a given denomination. This college is definitely and intimately church-related, though properly listed as private, meaning privately controlled, in college directories.

In still other instances, of course, colleges have drifted away from their original church relationships and in the end have separated themselves from the founding church, resorting at times to legal procedures to cut the "ties that bind." Such ties need not bind, in any undesirable sense, if wisdom and understanding operate. At the other extreme are those colleges whose trustees are elected by some church body or bodies, which have *ex-officio* church representation on the board, and which spell out denominational membership requirements for staff and faculty. There are occasional instances of direct supervision by some overhead church board, with quite rigid regulations as to administrative procedures. Such provisions, in my judgment, have at least the potential of handicapping and harassing a president, however loyal to his church he may be.

In sum, it seems to me that the terms of the charter of your college ensure the maintenance of the church relationship while providing the very generous measure of freedom that any college, and any board of trustees, ought to have. Under these broad charter provisions your concern now, as president, is to arrange for the most effective service of the board in furthering the purposes of the college and assuring its continuing development. This can, in part at least, be accomplished through a thoroughgoing revision of your bylaws.

I venture to suggest that, in advance of any actual rewriting, you arrange for a discussion by your board of the responsibilities of trustees. A full day might well be devoted to this procedure. An outside speaker, carefully chosen, might start the discussion, but your trustees should not be asked just to listen to a speech. You might ask some individual members of your board to read in advance some of the literature which I referred to in my earlier letter and report on their reading. Or, if some of them have attended meetings of the kind also referred to, ask them to report on the discussions that took place. In any case, every opportunity and incentive should be provided for question and comment and the expression of views on the part of your trustees.

Such a session may not be easy to arrange or to manage, but I am quite sure that it will be profitable if you can carry out some such plan. A small special committee can then be appointed to do the actual rewriting of the bylaws. Such a committee will have a background of insight into the task, which should guard them against the obvious dangers. Unsatisfactory bylaws are sometimes the product of a single author who simply incorporates his own ideas on organization and procedure. Sometimes the bylaws of a number of other institutions are used as models and a confusing composite is the result.

As a general principle I urge that your new bylaws be as simple and as free of restrictive details as is consistent with both efficiency and flexibility. Your present bylaws seem to me heavily overloaded with detail. Much that is in them could, I am sure, either be omitted, left to determination by the board as changing conditions warrant, or incorporated in other documents to be developed by the president and, when necessary, approved by the board. The present bylaws are not, I think, nearly so extreme in this respect as some I have seen; nevertheless, they greatly need simplification and streamlining.

As an extreme example of too much detail, one set of bylaws that I have seen fixes the dates for the opening and the closing of the college, making it necessary for the *board* to act if for any reason, as has often happened, these dates have to be changed. Incidentally, these particular bylaws, cluttered up as they are with a mass of detail, have been so frequently amended that the typed inserts in the official copy bulk almost as large as the original document. I am glad to add that these bylaws are now undergoing complete rewriting.

With some precision but without too much elaboration your bylaws should: designate the titles of the board's officers and outline the duties of each; designate the standing committees of the board and outline their duties; provide for the appointment of *ad hoc* committees as they may be needed; specify the number of regular meetings of the board and the approximate dates for such meetings, providing, of course, for the calling of special meetings as needed; establish a general order of business for meetings of the board; provide procedure for amending the bylaws.

There may of course be other things that your board will wish to include. Sometimes a board's bylaws specify some details relating to the administration of the college. If this is thought necessary, I suggest that such provisions be very general in character, so that organization and procedures can readily be adjusted to changing conditions. In many institutions, provisions for the administration of the college are incorporated in a separate document called the "bylaws of the college," or "administrative bylaws," as distinct from the bylaws of the board. Quite properly these bylaws go into greater detail about internal organization and procedure. But here again there are many details that are best left to determination by the administrative officers, with board approval when necessary.

For example, elaborate rules for faculty appointments, lengthy job specifications for administrative staff, salary scales, fringe benefits, faculty organization and the like need codification, but they ought to appear not as bylaws but in separate publications, handbooks or guides, subject to revision as circumstances may require.

With a board as large as yours, a good executive committee seems to me extremely important. There are certain dangers to be guarded against. Such a committee can be so small that authority is too narrowly concentrated. On the other hand the committee can be so large as to be unwieldy and to disperse the sense of responsibility unduly. The executive committee should, of course, be vested with authority to act *ad interim* for the board, but other members of the board should be kept informed of the committee's actions and those actions should be subject to formal approval by the full board when it meets.

I should, I think, note the fact that a good many colleges have boards much smaller than yours, with no more than five to nine members. Such boards can of course meet more frequently than a larger board, and the need for functioning through committees virtually disappears. It is also to be noted, though, that when the board itself is quite small it is often thought desirable to supplement the legally responsible board with an advisory board.

Sometimes the executive committee, to which I attach so much importance, is made up of the chairmen of several standing committees with special responsibilities. The chairman of the board should be, of course, a member of the executive committee and, I think, an *ex-officio* member of all other committees.

In my judgment the number of standing committees should be kept small and there should be provision both for continuity and for rotation of membership. The special interests and experience of individual trustees should be taken into account in making committee appointments. The committees should be large enough in membership to guard against too great a concentration of authority and small enough to insure regularity of meeting and proper attention to detail. Such committees may be made subcommittees of the executive committee or, better, their membership may interlock with the membership of the executive committee.

Among the standing committees most frequently encountered are those on educational policy, on finance or investment, on buildings and grounds, on nominations. You may think of others that would be helpful: on development, for example, or on public relations. But try to avoid having too many. Try also to avoid any overlapping or duplication of functions.

There are a good many other details regarding board organization and procedures about which I have some fairly definite opinions. I have, however, refrained from touching on them in this letter. If, as the redrafting of your bylaws goes forward, specific questions come up on which you might wish my comment, please call on me. As I have suggested, I hope there will be a chance later for some conference with you—and by conference I do not mean anything formal; simply an opportunity for informal talk about any details that may be of interest.

There is, however, one point on which I'd like to comment now. You mentioned in our conversation some concern about the average age of the members of your board as at present constituted. You'd like to bring in some younger men, some "fresh blood."

I'm afraid there's nothing you can do about this just now. The situation is not, I think, too bad, and in the natural course of events time will take care of it. I have only two suggestions. First, be on the lookout for younger men who are demonstrating the kind of capacity you will need when replacements are in order and, in appropriate ways, try to cultivate their interest. It is to be hoped that you will be consulted when nominations of new members are being considered, though of course you will not wish or be expected to handpick your board. Second, if you can find a way to do it without offense, try to get an age limit set for service as an active board member, with provision for emeritus status when the age of retirement is reached. Such status should carry the privilege of attendance and participation in discussion, without the right to vote. You probably should not make this rule apply to members already in service unless they, as individuals, request emeritus status, but it can be applied to those subsequently elected. I add that trustees emeriti can sometimes be most helpful if their interest continues. At the same time the way has been cleared for younger men.

It is a quite unusual opportunity you are having to work with your trustees in so thoroughgoing a revision of basic documents as seems to be contemplated. Once more I congratulate you and assure you of my continuing interest. Call on me when in any way I can be of service.

Sincerely,

# 4

## *Presidential Authority*

DEAR PRESIDENT HOSMER:

It was good to get such a frank, open letter from you. I sympathize with you in your seeming impasse. But let me assure you that your experience is by no means exceptional. In one way or another, I am sure, most college presidents have had their authority challenged by staff or faculty members at least once during their tenure of office. I am constantly running into it on my visits to colleges. Let me share with you a couple of experiences.

A president of my acquaintance had to face an open break with a staff member who had imagined a personal slight, quite unknown to the president. When invited to the president's office, the staff member refused, and when he was called again hung up the receiver. Being convinced that his authority was at stake and that the whole situation would deteriorate unless he acted with strength, the president wrote a letter demanding an interview but, after much thought and even prayer, decided to try persuasion. Using the "invincible, unconquerable good will" technique, the president kept the man on the staff, treated him as part of the community and sent him Christmas and birthday greetings. About four or five months later, when the president was returning from the city, a voice from the sidewalk asked for a ride. It turned out to be the recalcitrant staff member. During the ride back to the campus the member broke down completely, asked forgiveness and pledged unqualified loyalty. The transformation was complete and lasting.

In another instance, a department head had the habit of using his connections with influential alumni to gain favors for his department. The president explained that, in fairness to other departments and the total budget, it would be impossible to continue such favors. Again persuasion was used, but the result was as if one were talking to a blank wall. When it became evident that this method would not work, the president assumed the attitude of a military officer and issued a command. Somewhat to his surprise, the command was obeyed, and full compliance with his presidential authority was assured from that time on.

What conclusion would you draw? Surely that there is no such thing as a pat answer or a simple solution for the personal problems of administration. So much depends on the local situation, on the characters and personalities of the people involved. It seems to me that the best service I can render you is to review briefly the evolution of the authority of college presidents in this country, indicate the extremes to be avoided and try to identify a few guiding principles.

In colonial colleges, where the president gathered about him teachers and associates of his own choosing, he was effectively head of the team and made decisions in consultation with his colleagues. As colleges grew in size and complexity, a more formal organization developed. This called for a clear definition of purpose, a more definite program and a careful selection of administrators.

Ultimate responsibility for decisions is today placed by the board of trustees upon the president—even though the president cannot, in view of the influence exercised by others connected with the institution, have full control. He has power to delegate authority and is generally under pressure from the faculty to do so. It is desirable, however, to enlist the enthusiasm and support of his teammates, provided that he does not turn over to them the responsibility of his office. He must respect faculty tenure and academic freedom. While he may *delegate*, he cannot *abdicate* the authority given him. In some institutions, of course, there is legal provision for faculty participation in educational decisions, and this alters the position of the president in significant ways.

A wise president will not hesitate to receive advice and suggestions from his faculty, even when it is not mandatory; and they, in turn, will usually be satisfied to know that they have had a voice in shaping such policy as affects them. Teachers and staff are not so much concerned with final decisions as with being regularly consulted and having a say in the work of the college as a whole. As long as there is open give-and-take between the president and the faculty, and a continuing realization of the "bonds of fellowship" that hold them together, a happy and wholesome relationship can prevail. This is the ideal situation, but practice often falls short of the ideal.

Retired military officers, government or business executives who become college presidents are sometimes baffled by faculty "meddling" or opposition to authority in the administration of college or university affairs. It is said that one military man remarked soon after his election as president of a university: "What kind of a place is this? I give an order and nothing happens. People pay no attention to what I say, or reply that they will take it under advisement. I ask for an opinion on how to proceed, and I get fifty different opinions. I propose what I think is a capital idea, and it produces a faculty wrangle. How does a man get things done in a place like this?"

Commenting on presidential-faculty relationships, another president observed that the chief executive seemed to have power only to raise teachers' pay, improve pensions, provide less work, give more sabbaticals, get more money for buildings and equipment and arrange better parking facilities. As far as the routine of his office was concerned, he said, his job consisted of receiving reports, listening to complaints, referring to subordinates recommendations that disagreed with his own ideas, and asking a committee or a junior officer to make decisions that the president might approve. Since it is difficult for such presidents to make decisions—they don't like to fall back on rubber-stamping—they tend to set up barriers between themselves and the individuals and groups that press them for special consideration. They establish a secretarial guard, keep themselves pretty much to themselves, water down speeches and public comments until they become either innocuous or ambiguous, and spend more and more time off campus, attending national organizations or making speeches to patriotic societies.

Any president is almost certain, sooner or later, to be characterized as an autocrat—or alternatively to be charged with letting his authority slip away from him, through permitting others to make decisions that he alone should make. He may at different times, or even simultaneously, be subject to both charges.

The delegation of authority is one of the most difficult and delicate of the arts of administration. It is peculiarly so in educational administration because of the fact that major administrative officers must be interested in the *total* life of the college, and the functions recognized as focusing in one area of responsibility inevitably affect other areas. It thus becomes much more difficult than it is in any sizable business organization to draw sharp lines of division separating the authority of different officers.

Different individuals accept responsibility and exercise authority in different ways; they differ also in their attitudes toward their chief. Some enjoy throwing their weight around, tend to become little "empire builders," and resent any necessity for clearing with or reporting to a superior. Others are hesitant to make decisions, require too much advance approval, and too much backing and encouragement from the top executive. Things don't get done because of this hesitancy to take the initiative, to assume responsibility, to exercise authority. To make effective use of staff members falling in some measure into one or other of these two categories, particularly when they must work as a team, taxes the administrative skill of a president.

But it is also true that some of the difficulty often roots in the disposition of the president himself. As he is ultimately responsible for everything, he may find it exceedingly difficult at times to let go of details, let alone major activities. Even where he has an effective associate to whom much might be entrusted, he is still disposed to keep too tight a rein, to ask too many trivial questions, to make too many unimportant suggestions. In extreme cases one encounters a president who trusts no one, who makes *all* the decisions. In one college of more than a thousand students, I found the president making decisions on details of buildings and grounds, budgetary and accounting procedures, standards of admission, course offerings, student discipline, college-community relations, fund raising and investments.

There may be advantages for a college in the dominating type of president who can keep his hand on a multiplicity of details, call all the shots, run the whole show, particularly if he can rally round him a group of loyal and enthusiastic devotees. But, sooner or later, such a president is likely to find himself with a docile and submissive faculty—or with an antagonistic and rebellious one—or with a mixture of the two. And when he goes, as in time he must, his successor will face grievous problems. The institution built around the personality of one man is sure to run into trouble when someone else has to take over; the history of some of our best-known institutions furnishes illustrations. A difficult period of complete rebuilding is often necessary, and the process is bound to be slow and costly.

All this is simply to suggest that keeping the balance between autocracy, on the one hand, with its direct and effective exercise of authority, and on the other hand, a loosely organized regime in which authority is too widely dispersed, and confusion and uncertainty ensue—keeping this balance will be one of your most fundamental problems. To change the metaphor, you will have to steer a middle course between the two extremes, relying now on the force of command, now on the power of persuasion.

In short, the president should communicate fully with all the members of his team; should strive to delegate as large a share as possible of his authority; should accord a generous measure of responsibility to his associates; and should provide encouragement to all who participate in the college enterprise. At the same time, he must let it be known, by action rather than words, that a government exists and that a responsible man is at the helm, a man who knows where he is going and why. He must have a plan of action and be able to articulate and share his hopes. It is important to have a clearly stated set of objectives, a well-organized program, a carefully selected staff and an understanding and dedicated faculty. But, in the last analysis, the president must be willing to make his own decisions and to take responsibility for the consequences.

Keep up your courage! With calmness, integrity and a good measure of patience, you will succeed. You have the talent and energy to do the job, and you have a good team to help you. So you can afford to be generous when confronted with opposition. In a situation like the present one, just talk it over quietly and frankly with the individuals who are causing the trouble. Long-drawn-out discussions and maneuvers tend to complicate rather than clarify such situations, but with patience and persistence a common ground of understanding can usually be found. If not, you must act with firmness and decision. By so doing, you will win respect and strengthen your position for the future.

Sincerely,

# 5

## *Some Principles of Administration*

DEAR AUBREY:

It was a privilege to have your visit the other day. I am now looking forward with real eagerness to visiting you soon on your new campus. I shall be very much interested in seeing the progress on your new buildings for which you showed me the plans.

As you know, I am deeply impressed by your decision to give up a successful career in the legal profession to accept this challenging opportunity for an important contribution to higher education. You are coming to the presidency of what is actually a new college, though it inherits much fine tradition from the colleges that are merging to form this new one. The situation is unusual, almost unique. In large measure, this clears the way for you to project your own plans. At the same time, some problems and difficulties may grow out of the necessity for conserving something of the old while projecting the new. These problems may at times tax your patience. Certainly they will make heavy demands on your time and energy.

I know that you have conferred with a number of others and that by this time you may have had a surfeit of advice and conflicting opinions. I hope I will not add unduly to any confusion you may be feeling.

My first word now is simply this: Take everything in stride. Resolve from the start to pace yourself and to conserve your health and strength. This may not be easy. There will be many things you want to do. But your continuing effectiveness on the job is more important than getting everything done at once.

This exhortation from an old-timer who has been through the mill may seem overly paternal. Actually I write this letter to fulfill my promise to send you in writing, in ordered fashion, some of the ideas that emerged as we talked about the question that was then uppermost in your mind: the question of your administrative organization. Faculty organization and faculty participation in administration came into our discussion, but I leave these questions for another time and speak now only of your full-time administrative staff.

I have found myself thinking about the much greater complexity of college administration today as compared with earlier times. Most of the added demands on the president and his staff have come about within the last fifteen or twenty years. But I cannot help going still further back to my own undergraduate days which, as you know, fell within the first decade of this century.

The president of my college at that time had only a part-time secretary who served also as assistant librarian. The president wrote most of his letters by hand. The librarian was a faculty member who taught a full load and also helped the president with some of the business details. There was no dean. The faculty had a secretary who would now be called registrar; he too taught full time. And that was "the administration." I am not suggesting that the president of those days had an easy job. Some of his problems would break the heart, if not the back, of a modern college president. I suggest only that fifty or sixty years ago college administration was virtually a one-man operation.

The fact that the college I attended was small accounts only in slight measure for its administrative simplicity. Administering that same college today (it is larger, but not much) is a highly complicated job. This is due, I think, chiefly to the changes that have occurred in the total pattern of American higher education. Many of these changes have resulted from changes in American life and from the more intimate relationships of the college to the complex structures of government and of society in general. To cite just one example, almost no college, however small, escapes the exacting necessity of dealing with the Federal Government: income tax withholding and reporting, social security payments, administering Federal loan funds for students, and so forth.

Thus, even in a small college the administration is not and cannot be just the president and two or three part-time helpers. There must be a staff of full-time officers with varied but interrelated responsibilities. They must work together as a team under the captaincy of the president. Each must be an expert, or, I should prefer to say, highly competent in his special field, yet able and willing to relate and even subordinate his own particular expertise to the over-all purposes of the college and to the policies and procedures agreed upon under the leadership of the president.

I think it may be helpful, against this general background, to state certain principles that seem to me basic to good administrative organization and procedure. I suggest these five for your consideration:

1. There must be clearly understood differentiation of function and of correlative responsibility and authority for the various administrative officers.

2. There must, at the same time, be recognition of interrelationships and of some actual overlapping of areas of responsibility. This may sometimes result in confusion or even conflict. The president may at times have to resolve issues of this kind, and it is well to have it understood that he expects to maintain a measure of flexibility in the borderline areas.

3. There must be cooperation in attitude and in procedure. This implies mutual respect and confidence among members of the administrative staff. Regularly scheduled meetings of this group with the president will contribute greatly to the sharing of information and to understanding. Such meetings can often be quite brief; at other times, when major issues are under consideration, discussion may have to be prolonged. In any case, I am sure that getting together regularly is most helpful. None of this, of course, rules out the possibility of disagreement. But it leaves no

excuse for petty jealousies, personal animosities, smoldering resentments and "sulking in one's tent."

4. There must be understanding of and commitment to the stated purposes of the institution. This implies recognition of the fact that all the activities of the administrative officers must be carried on in the service of those purposes, whether the activities are *directly* related to their accomplishment or whether they seem to be auxiliary in nature.

5. There must be a basic loyalty to the president, because he is the responsible leader of the enterprise in which each of his associates cooperates and to which each should be dedicated. Again, this does not rule out disagreement. It does not imply the necessity for personal admiration or affection, though these are certainly not ruled out. They may exist without the slightest implication of subservience or sycophancy. The essential point is that when there is disagreement it should be openly expressed in free and frank discussion. There is no excuse for sulking, political maneuvering, undercover nurturing of support for one's personal animosities, or subtle undermining of confidence in the president. If deep-seated distrust or personal antagonism persists, a parting of the ways is proper and inevitable.

These principles are of course very general. Perhaps they are so obvious as to seem hardly worth writing out. Nevertheless they are all too often little understood or deliberately ignored or violated. I am sure that if you are able to muster in a staff whose members understand and accept such statements and their implications, your administration will be more successful and happier than it otherwise might be.

Now, Aubrey, this letter is already long enough, and I have an engagement I must keep. I had intended to include some suggestions of a specific kind as to the top-level associates whom, in my judgment, you will need. This will have to wait for another letter. I promise you it will not be long delayed.

Meantime my continuing regards and good wishes. I can't refrain from saying again: Take care of yourself.

Sincerely,

# 6

## *The President's Chief Administrative Associates*

DEAR AUBREY:

This is the follow-up I promised in my letter of two days ago. With no further introduction I will get directly to the question of what top-level administrative staff you will need.

The two most generally recognized areas in which a president needs highly competent lieutenants are academic affairs and business affairs. You will then, I suggest, be first concerned with the appointment of administrative officers with major responsibility in each of these two fields. You will need an *academic dean* and a *business manager*. You may wish to give them somewhat different titles, but a word or two on that point later.

It may be that for the present you can stop there, making all other members of the administrative staff directly responsible to one or the other of these two officers. You would then have only two administrative associates in the top echelon, only two people directly responsible to you.

But this will probably not suffice for an institution which is in process of development and which you expect to grow rather rapidly in the years just ahead. A student body of the size you anticipate will require much more in the way of extracurricular or, as they are sometimes called, "co-curricular" services than does a college small enough for everybody to know everybody else.

Then, too, your constituency and the general public must be kept informed about your plans and your programs; you must in time have much larger endowment and greatly increased income from annual contributions for current operating expenses. Of this you are well aware, and you are already devoting a good deal of your time to public speaking and to the making of contacts. In this whole important area you will need competent help.

Thus you will probably need two additional staff members on the top level. They will be concerned: (1) with student personnel work—supervision and guidance of the life of students outside the classroom, library and laboratory; (2) with public relations and development. You will be looking for a *dean of students* and a *director of public relations*. Again I defer comment on alternative titles as well as attempts at interpretation of the relationships and responsibilities of these officers.

You will have, then, if these suggestions are sound, *four* top-level administrative associates. I venture to hope that for a good long time this will suffice for this echelon of your administrative organization. But your planning will of course have to go quite a bit further than provision for this level.

You will need a librarian. You will need a registrar. You will need a director of admissions, who may be, for a time, the registrar as well, though I think that very soon you will have to divide the responsibility in these two related fields. You will, I am sure, want a college chaplain or a director of religious life. There will be need for additional competent personnel in the area of business management almost from the beginning and, in time, in the other areas as well.

How will you organize your staff to bring the now rather numerous officers into satisfactory relationship with one another, so that unnecessary misunderstandings are avoided and no one of them is just "hanging loose"? It is important that the number of officers directly responsible to you as president be held down to the maximum already indicated or to some number close to that maximum.

There is, of course, no one right answer. The answer you finally come up with will depend in part on your own preferences and perhaps in even larger measure on the people available and responsive to the invitation to join you in carrying forward your plans for the college.

I am sure you have already looked at a good many organization charts, and you may have studied manuals that incorporate more or less elaborate job specifications. I have found these devices useful in my own work and in getting an understanding of the operations of some of the colleges I have visited, but useful only up to a point. I think they can be overdone. A beautiful organization chart and elaborate job specifications really guarantee nothing. They tell one little about how the administrative organization actually works. Why? Because the effectiveness of any administration is dependent on the *people* who make up the team.

If this seems a trite statement, forgive me. I cannot refrain from making it, because I have known too many instances in which one man was causing the breakdown of what, on its face, should have been an efficient, smooth-running administrative setup. It is people who must work the plan, however carefully the plan is charted. It is people who must do the jobs the details of which may have been carefully specified. The wrong people can wreck any organizational pattern. Maybe I don't need to say all this to you, but I say it anyway because I feel it so strongly.

If, as you go forward with your planning, you find that your own charts and job analyses are helpful, by all means use them. But don't let them rob you of the freedom you should have to make adjustments as you go along. Don't let them deprive your organization of the flexibility that, on occasion, may enable you to avoid some serious lapses or conflicts.

What follows is an attempt to suggest some of the possible variations in the organizational pattern and some of the interrelationships of the suggested areas of responsibility. I do not need to say, I am sure, that I am not trying to *prescribe* for you. At the same time, I am not trying to hide my own preferences, even though they may be out of line with some current tendencies or with advice others may have given you.

I do not think the question of titles for your major administrative officers is of critical importance. I recall that in our recent conversation you indicated a leaning toward the idea of getting away from the conventional or generally used titles and adopting such titles as "Chief Academic Officer," "Chief Business Officer" and so on, though just what the "and so on" would involve I am not sure.

Let me take up each of the major officers in order. In the area of academic responsibility I much prefer the title "Dean of the College." Alternatives would be "Dean of the Faculty" or "Dean of Instruction." In any case I would want him to be *Dean*.

This is a vitally important office—the most important, I think, in relation to the basic educational objectives of the college. The college deanship can be reduced to the level of a clerkship. It should not be. It can and should be a position of educational leadership.

I note, incidentally, that while in recent years there has been much writing, including a number of books, on the college or university presidency, there is a scarcity of careful studies of the college deanship. In fact I know of only two books devoted exclusively to discussion of this office. Both are quite small; one of them is not well known, the other has been published very recently. There are, of course, relevant chapters or sections in books on college administration, and the educational journals provide occasional articles dealing with the dean's problems. What is greatly needed is a thoroughgoing study of what college deans actually do, what they should do, and their relationships to the president, to other administrative officers, to the faculty and to the students.

I must content myself now with emphasizing the fact that mutual confidence and complete understanding between the president and the dean are absolutely essential. I emphasize the president-dean relationship because I have seen a regrettable number of situations in which mutual trust and understanding were lacking, for one reason or another, with the result that the whole educational operation was confused or dragging.

I think the college librarian should be made directly responsible to the dean. All faculty chairmen, whether of divisions or of departments, are obviously directly responsible to the dean. In my judgment, the registrar and the director of admissions should also be responsible to the academic dean or dean of the college. There is a current tendency to relate these two officers to the dean of students, on the ground that they are concerned with student personnel affairs. Of course they are; but admissions and student records involve chiefly academic matters and in my view should be under the direct supervision of the academic dean, not the dean of students. This is a pretty good illustration of the overlapping of functions and of the difficulty of drawing sharp lines. Cooperative relationships between the two deans should be established and maintained, of course. As a matter of fact, it is not at all unusual to find the dean of students himself made responsible to the dean of the college.

Sometimes the responsibility and authority of the dean of the college is still further broadened and he becomes, in effect, second in command. He may indeed be given the additional title of vice president. Sometimes the title "provost" is used, though usually in large and complex institutions. Certainly I am not suggesting these additional titles for your use at this time. I am chiefly concerned with emphasizing the prime importance of the academic deanship. I hope you may find just the right man.

I have one other suggestion. Many a president has found it most helpful to have closely related to him, in addition to these major administrative officers, an assistant to the president (not, I hardly need to say, an assistant president). This assistant must have ability, understanding and tact, a knack of getting along with all kinds of people, a willingness to do a variety of routine things, even a willingness to assume at times responsibility without authority. He must be more than a secretary or a clerk. He may be a mature man with experience, good judgment and genuinely superior abilities, but without an academic background that justifies his appointment to top-level administrative office. Perhaps he should have what one of our country's presidents characterized as a "passion for anonymity." Possibly he should have all the qualities just suggested but also, as one

college president said of the man he was looking for, "no ambition."

It is more likely that this assistant will be a young man who
is on the way up and whom the president cannot expect to keep
indefinitely. In that case, a succession of young men can be
given an apprenticeship in administration, on the basis of which
they may move into more responsible or more honorific administrative posts. At the same time, if they are brought from the
junior ranks of the faculty into administration in the capacity
suggested, the way for their return to teaching without loss of
status should be ensured.

I think it likely that such an assistant can be highly valuable
to you. Many presidents, of whom I am one, can express gratitude and a sense of deep obligation for such help.

Enough for this time. I have still touched only on certain selected details relating to the organization of your administrative
staff. I think, however, that they are among the details that need
to be highlighted. You may have further questions on which
you would like my opinion. If so, please feel free to write. I am
interested and I want to be of service in any way I can.

Sincerely,

# 7

## Administration-Faculty Relationships

DEAR PRESIDENT BRONSON:

Since returning from my visit with you last week, I have been reflecting on your problem of faculty morale. This matter deserves more extended analysis than we were able to give it in our few minutes of discussion on the way to the airport. I agree with you that it is as urgent as any problem you face, and it must be solved, or at least alleviated, if your faculty and staff are to move forward as a team. While I am sure you are not overly concerned about your personal popularity (no president who is doing his job can be popular with everybody), it is important that you have the confidence and trust of your faculty. In my judgment, no one thing is more essential to the welfare of the institution and to your personal satisfaction as president.

Some degree of strain in the relationships between faculty and administration seems to be almost universal in American colleges. It is perhaps inherent in our pattern of organization, which places the president in the position of having to reconcile the sometimes divergent views and expectations of a lay board of trustees, on the one hand, and of a professional teaching staff, on the other. From my observations at many colleges, however, I am confident there are steps you can take to improve relationships at your own institution.

In my conversations with members of your faculty I tried to explore, as tactfully as I could, their attitude toward you as president. I did not, of course, ask direct questions but encouraged any comments that might be volunteered. I am glad to report that there seems to be no deep-seated antagonism or distrust. Your aspirations for the college and your devoted work are acknowledged and appreciated. There were, however, indications of considerable anxiety and dissatisfaction. Criticism was directed toward "the administration," not toward you personally. Many members of the faculty feel they are not "on the inside." As they put it, "We just don't know what's going on."

Before considering specific measures, let's look at the background of the problem. You came to the presidency with full knowledge that for several years the college had lacked vigor and a sense of direction. There were serious financial difficulties. The educational program was obviously lacking in vitality. Coming from the outside, you had to devote most of your first year to getting acquainted—with the trustees, the faculty, the alumni, the students, the community. You accepted almost daily invitations to address all kinds of gatherings. This kept you out of your office and away from the campus much of the time. I think you should now be more selective in accepting invitations and concentrate on occasions and audiences that are really important. (Most college presidents make too many speeches.) This will conserve your time and energy and enable you to give more attention to the faculty.

Even with these heavy demands of the first year, you have dealt effectively, I think, with the problems relating to finance and business management. You may have seemed at times a bit ruthless and somewhat overconcerned to have your authority recognized in these areas. Perhaps some of the reorganization could have been accomplished more tactfully. But it had to be done. Since such changes affect the teaching staff only indirectly, their influence on faculty attitudes has probably been negligible.

*But*—here is the really significant factor—you are now well into the second year of your administration, pushing hard for the *educational reforms* to which you are committed. At this point I am not concerned with the changes themselves but with the procedure followed in bringing them about and with the effect of such procedure on your faculty relationships. Some senior members of the faculty have the impression that you are reluctant to submit your proposals to faculty discussion and criticism. Your feeling of urgency is understandable, but in this area of college affairs the faculty is directly involved, typically jealous of its prerogatives, and quite unwilling to have any new plan handed down with the implied obligation to take it and like it, or get out.

Perhaps I exaggerate. I am sure it is not your intent to be arbitrary. But I do urge on you the importance of patience in effecting curricular revision. You may not, in the end, get quite all you want. But if the faculty comes up finally with a plan that is *theirs*, even though many of the ideas were originally *yours*, the new plan is far more likely to vitalize the institution, as you wish it vitalized, than if the changes were imposed by administrative fiat. The reason is, I think, obvious: the faculty, as well as the president, will be committed.

I know that faculty discussion and debate are not always conducted on a high level of wisdom and unselfishness. Often they degenerate into petty disagreement or acrimonious controversy. They may involve departmental log rolling and horse trading. Even so, decisions emerging from such discussions are more likely to be constructive and lasting than are decisions imposed on a rebellious or submissive faculty.

I know also that, even in the best of colleges, faculty discussion can sometimes be trivial and time-wasting. The "town-meeting" idea, with everybody deciding everything, is not a good pattern for faculty deliberation. All of us have witnessed the spectacle, in colleges or elsewhere, of highly trained people frittering away their time quibbling over details.

In your faculty of seventy-five people, it would be wise to delegate detailed educational planning to a smaller, carefully chosen, representative body, which might be called the Senate or Academic Council. I think the academic dean should be *ex-officio* chairman, and there might well be other *ex-officio* members. Some of the members should be elected by the faculty for stipulated terms, with provision for rotation. A total membership of twelve or fifteen would seem about right. Regular reports by this body, or distribution of the minutes of its meetings to the general faculty, would help to obviate criticisms of star chamber proceedings.

Such a senate or council can save the time of full faculty meetings for consideration of larger questions. In relatively minor matters (e.g., approval of new courses, granting permission for exceptions to requirements), such a body should have final authority. It might well, in turn, delegate some authority to still smaller subcommittees, in order to clear its own agenda for less routine business. In matters of major importance (e.g., a thoroughgoing revision of the curriculum, the setting up of honors programs, a drastic reorganization of the academic calendar) the senate or council can do the intensive study necessary for the development of sound proposals for presentation to the general faculty. In the course of its deliberations, it should let other faculty members know what is under consideration and provide opportunity for interested persons not on the council to be heard. I add that my own conviction is that there should also be, in any case, the right of appeal to the faculty as a whole from the decisions of this delegated body.

I hope I have not conveyed the impression that general faculty meetings are unimportant. They serve a good purpose in promoting *esprit de corps* and should be held periodically for consideration of committee reports and discussion of broad educational policy.

Let me say, also, that I am decidedly *not* suggesting the abdication by the president of responsibility for the educational program. In my judgment, despite all the other demands made upon him, this is the most significant of his responsibilities. But in this area, above all others, he must *lead* and *guide,* not command. Explanation, persuasion, interpretation, inspiration—at times, perhaps, concession and compromise—are needed if a faculty is to commit itself to the educational program in wholehearted fashion. And cherished plans of the president in academic areas must, I think, run the gauntlet of faculty discussion and be subjected to all the hazards of that procedure if they are to have in the end any real viability and vitality.

I add one other point in this connection which might appear, but is not actually, inconsistent with the principle I have been urging. In my judgment, all faculty action should be subject to the final approval of the president. On this point there may be some disagreement, but it seems to me essential in the structure of the American college. In any case, a wise president would be reluctant to disapprove faculty action taken after full discussion, in academic areas, and would carefully explain to the faculty his reasons if such disapproval were, in his judgment, necessary.

Through the procedure I have outlined, your relationships with your faculty should improve, because you will have shared with them responsibility and authority in matters in which they are deeply concerned.

Now, before bringing this already long letter to a close, I want to comment on a few lesser points.

"We don't know what's going on." This, I think, simply reflects a normal human attitude. Everybody likes to be "in the know," "on the inside." I suggest only that this wish on the part of a faculty must be recognized, and its dangers guarded against as fully as possible. For example, it should be established policy to convey to the faculty information about matters of importance well in advance of public announcement. Sometimes, for good reasons, this can't be done. Occasionally there will be leaks or premature news stories before information reaches the faculty. In these circumstances, the only thing the president can do is to explain to the faculty how it happened and to make clear *his* wish to have the faculty informed first.

Communication, to the end of keeping the faculty informed is, then, vitally important. Formal oral and written reports to the faculty at appropriate intervals and in considerable detail are valuable. The reports should deal with pending developments, with important actions of the governing board, with new appointments to the faculty, and the like. Opportunity should also be provided for individual faculty members to offer suggestions and ask questions.

But formal communication is not sufficient. You need to develop happy informal relationships too. I am not thinking of the conventional faculty receptions, teas, dinners, etc. These serve a good purpose, especially if they include talks by the president or by visiting scholars on educational subjects of import. But they do not take the place of the almost casual contacts on the campus or the drop-in visits to, or by, the president. There are hazards, of course, on which I could elaborate. Still, the president should make it understood that any member of the institution from the janitor up can have access to him if necessary.

I have never seen how the "ever open door" to the president's office could possibly work, though it has been the practice of some presidents I have known. But the president should not allow *artificial* barriers to create an impression of inaccessibility. Most important is a pleasing reception at your office, a gracious and friendly response to a drop-in call or to a telephone request for an appointment. I am sure that your efficient secretary feels that one of her duties is to protect you against unwarranted demands on your time but, from some remarks I have heard, it might be well to discuss with her how this can be done most tactfully.

I do not need to suggest to *you* the value of friendly personal notes on special occasions, as when a new honor has been received by a faculty member or his wife or a child. This should be followed by a personal word when the faculty member is next encountered. Then, of course, there are written or spoken words of sympathy in illness or bereavement. Such things mean more than you may realize. I am not suggesting overly effusive expressions. Nor, certainly, do I recommend an artificial routine. A certain measure of reserve can properly be associated with a genuine interest in your faculty and the faculty families as people.

The impersonal references to "the administration," of which I made passing mention earlier, may not deserve further comment. But I see in the usage meanings that have at times worried me. It may simply imply a wish to avoid direct criticism of the president. It can also suggest distrust or suspicion of the president's administrative associates, especially in nonacademic areas such as business administration.

And one thing more: the reference to the impersonal "administration" sometimes seems to hint that the president himself doesn't know "what's going on." I used to wish and sometimes to ask that I, the president, be referred to so that I could personally take the responsibility for whatever might be wrong. Implied here, of course, is the necessity for the president's administrative colleagues to keep him informed of what's going on.

I hope that these observations and suggestions will be useful to you in solving the problem of faculty morale. If I can be of further assistance, please let me know.

Sincerely,

# 8

## *Faculty Appointments,*
## *Rank and Promotion*

DEAR PRESIDENT SMYTHE:

I must confess my surprise at learning that you do not have codified procedures for dealing with faculty appointments, rank or promotion. It seems to me that clear understandings on these matters are very important. Knowing that you are now anxious to establish such procedures, I shall be pleased to assist in any way I can. I am glad to share with you whatever I have learned from my own experience and from conversations with presidents of your sister colleges.

Procedures differ somewhat from college to college. Thus there are still some of the smaller colleges where the president assumes responsibility for all the details of recruiting, interviewing and engagement of new faculty members. Necessarily, of course, he will work in consultation with the dean and the respective department heads. But in most colleges the finding of new faculty members has become such a chore that many people must join in the search, and the president must delegate initial responsibility to someone else.

Faculty openings must be anticipated well in advance of the actual need, so that there will be adequate opportunity to find possible candidates and to screen them properly. Usually it is the head of a department or a division (depending on the type of organization) who will first become aware of prospective vacancies or the need for additional teachers. Certainly he should apprise the academic dean of the situation and then, if he has the initial responsibility, go to work on the correspondence and telephone calls that are expected to uncover prospective candidates. Any department or division head will undoubtedly have contacts in his field at graduate schools.

If the going is difficult, it may be that the dean and the president can be called on to use such contacts as they may have with the deans of graduate schools. Even the fact that the department head has the initial responsibility is no reason why at this stage of the procedure he should hesitate to call on the dean and the president to help out if they can. This is no time to stand on protocol. In a small college, the responsibility of finding new faculty members may rest equally on the president, the dean and the department head.

In law, the authority for both appointment and promotion of faculty members vests in the board of trustees upon the nomination or recommendation of the president. Usually this power is substantially delegated to the president, and the results of his activity are simply reported to the board of trustees for confirmation. In any event, it is generally conceded that the president has the prime responsibility for building up the faculty of the college. No matter what procedure may be in vogue in a particular college, the president cannot completely abdicate his responsibility in the selection of faculty members. Even with most favorable reports from department or division head and dean, the president will wish to satisfy himself that the prospective faculty member meets all the requirements.

In this process, written information should be required, including a biography, educational background, teaching experience and adequate references. Any apparent gaps in the record should be checked and contacts made with references. Unfortunately, letter references are not always reliable. Where there is any vagueness about a letter, try if possible to make personal contact with the writer through interview or by telephone.

If the candidate passes the first stage of inquiry satisfactorily, the next step is the personal interview. If at all possible, this should take place at the college when the prospective teacher can spend a day there, in order to see for himself the campus and buildings, to meet and talk with the chairman and members of the department in which he would be expected to serve, and to meet and talk with members of the administration, including the president, who has final say on the appointment.

Appointments are either probationary, for a specified period, or continuous. Continuous appointments imply tenure, on which, in the circumstances you describe, I had better write you a separate letter. Most first appointments to a particular college are "term"—probationary in character—although there may be exceptions. In order to avoid later misunderstanding and difficulty, the precise terms and conditions of *every* appointment should be stated in writing and should be in the possession of both the college and the prospective faculty member before the appointment is settled.

All this seems to me to be procedure that would ordinarily be followed in any college exercising care in the building up of a faculty. Following this procedure for faculty appointments, there should also be definite policies on rank and promotion.

I am assuming that, like most colleges, you recognize distinctions of rank in your faculty. This means that you should without question have a published policy. Much trouble would be avoided if we did not have to bother with rank. I know of one or two four-year colleges which recognize no distinction in rank. Enviable as the courage and independence of these colleges may be, I doubt that the practice will spread.

Your published policy should, I suggest, set forth the ranks that are recognized and the qualifications and conditions necessary to attain each rank. In advance of such publication, however, two fundamental questions ought to be settled: (1) Has the college reduced the number of its academic departments to a workable minimum consistent with the size of the college and the size of its faculty? This means, among other things, doing away with the catalogue fiction of one-man or two- and three-men departments. (2) Since rank is closely tied to salary as well as to length of service, approximately what number of professors and associate professors in a given department can a college of moderate size and limited budget afford to have? At least it ought to be recognized that there will have to be some over-all limitation on the number of faculty members in the higher ranks.

Large institutions strive to keep a balance by fixing a more or less arbitrary time limit on the employment of faculty members in the lower ranks. Thus an instructor is automatically separated from the university faculty if, after a specified number of years of service, there is no opportunity for promotion to a vacant assistant professorship.

This policy does not seem to be either practicable or necessary for the average college. Sometimes good teachers are concerned more with the congeniality of their work at a small college than with rank. They may be willing to stay permanently without any definite assurance of advancement in rank, provided that tenure and improvement in salary are not thereby jeopardized. For that reason, in a small college, neither salary scale nor tenure ought to be too closely tied to rank.

In determining ranks, colleges customarily make a clear-cut distinction between full-time and part-time faculty members. Only full-time faculty members are considered eligible for rank. Part-time faculty members are not ranked but are often accorded the title of "lecturer." In ascending order, the ranks usually granted to full-time faculty members are: instructor, assistant professor, associate professor and professor. Some colleges do not have the rank of associate professor.

It is desirable, I think, that a college should have an established set of minimum requirements for each rank. In ordinary circumstances these minimum requirements should be observed, but there may be occasions when exceptions ought to be made. Unusual circumstances may arise in which an exception is in the best interests of the college. In such circumstances, the president and governing board should be able and willing to make an exception.

Let me, before commenting on such exceptions, suggest for your consideration the following minimum requirements for the various ranks. *Instructor:* At least a bachelor's degree or its equivalent, and indication that one has begun work for the master's degree. Although preferred, teaching experience is not essential. *Assistant Professor:* At least a master's degree or its equivalent, and indication that one has begun work for the doctor's degree; a total of five years' successful college teaching, of which at least three years should have been spent at the college in question. *Associate Professor:* A doctor's degree or its equivalent; at least five years of successful teaching in the rank of assistant professor, at least three years of it at the college in question; some evidence of scholarly attainment and superior ability as a teacher. *Professor:* A doctor's degree or its equivalent; at least five years of successful teaching in the rank of associate professor, at least three years of it at the college in question; undoubted evidence of scholarly attainments and outstanding ability as a teacher.

Now as to exceptions. These minimum requirements should not be considered so inflexible that the president and governing board would be unable, or would hesitate, to make exceptions when the interests of the college so required. For example, an outstandingly able teacher with less than the specified length of experience might nevertheless be promoted, or might be brought into the faculty at a higher level than that indicated by the minimum requirements. There may be good reasons why an import from another institution should be initially appointed to an associate or full professorship, even with tenure, despite his lack of previous experience at the college to which he is being appointed.

There may also be occasions when degree requirements as specified can be waived because of unusual qualifications of a different kind, or because of variant types of professional training and experience, as happens, for example, in the fine arts. None of this is intended, however, to detract from the desirability of having established minimum requirements for rank as the normal guide lines for advancement.

In considering the promotion of a faculty member to a higher rank there are, of course, other qualifications which ought to be evaluated, particularly in a small college in which teamwork is necessary: loyalty to the college as demonstrated by willingness to serve beyond the call of duty; devotion to the declared ideals of the college as shown by willingness to abide by those ideals and to promote them as far as possible in students; interest in students as evinced by a willingness to give personal assistance, where necessary, and to confer and counsel with them as may be required; willingness to cooperate with administration and faculty by faithfully serving on committees, attending faculty meetings and sharing such administrative tasks as may be assigned from time to time.

It is advisable, when you publish your statement of requirements, to make it clear that advancement to a higher rank does not necessarily follow when one has fulfilled the requirements prescribed for that particular rank. In other words, advancement to higher rank is not automatic. Three other conditions must be fulfilled. There must (except in unusual circumstances) be a vacancy in the rank to which advancement is sought. There must be a recommendation through the proper channels testifying that the candidate for advancement has met the established norms. Finally, there should be such approval by the president or governing board as may be required in the bylaws of the college.

It is usually preferable that requests or recommendations for promotion originate with the department chairman in written form and be channeled through a faculty committee on promotion, if there is one, to the dean and the president. Final approval will rest with the president if he has been delegated this authority by the board of trustees; otherwise it will depend on the board itself.

I am sure you will agree that definite published policies in these areas of faculty relationship are conducive to the satisfaction and peace of mind of faculty members. From the administrative point of view, they are of value in contributing to stability and orderly procedure. They guard against misunderstanding and conflict.

If I can be of further assistance when you have made the preliminary draft of your own policies, I will be happy to do what I can.

Sincerely,

# 9

## Tenure and Termination
## of Appointments

DEAR PRESIDENT SMYTHE:

If I were you I would not be greatly disturbed by the petition of your faculty group for a published policy on tenure. Other presidents have had similar experiences.

Only recently I encountered much the same situation at a college of moderate enrollment where I was visiting. The president explained that his college had no explicit tenure policy because there had been no apparent need for it. The college was small, the faculty pretty stable. New faculty members were selected with great care, chiefly from graduate schools. The occasional misfits in the relatively small faculty were readily detected in the first year or two. Thereafter, the president said, those who left the college did so of their own volition, usually to accept better offers elsewhere. In fact, the president told me, he knew of no instance in the past twenty years where the service of a faculty member who had been with the college for as long as three years had been terminated by the administration.

The board of trustees of this college recently decided to enlarge the student body and build another residence hall. Accordingly, several additions were made to the faculty. These new members, fresh from graduate school, were responsible for reactivating the dormant AAUP Chapter. The first tangible

57

result was a petition urging adoption and publication of a college policy on faculty tenure. Almost identical with your own situation, is it not?

In considering problems of tenure, the basic fact to be borne in mind is that professors pretty consistently—and I think, rightly—maintain that they are not employees of the college in the sense that tellers are employees of a bank or salesmen of a business firm. The American college has never approximated very closely to the academic ideal of a self-governing community of scholars, like the medieval university, in which the teaching body was itself the corporation. Nevertheless, it is fairly widely recognized by thoughtful people that a college or university is a different kind of entity from any other social institution. The faculty stands in a unique relationship to the corporate body, because its activities constitute the *raison d'être* of the whole enterprise and are not just an assortment of services performed by hired hands under the direction of the management.

This unique relationship gives rise to an equally exceptional pattern of rights and obligations. I cannot attempt to develop in a letter the full consequences of this line of reasoning, but one of its implications is important for our immediate purpose. If professors are not mere employees but an integral part of the institution, they should not need such legal devices as have been found generally necessary to protect employees against unjust and arbitrary treatment by their employers. Ideally, such protective measures should be irrelevant to the academic situation. And, in practice, I believe you will find that the better the grasp a college has of the nature of its mission, the less often is it necessary for members of its faculty to look for protection to some kind of "Bill of Rights."

Unfortunately, however, this peculiar characteristic of the academic institution is not universally understood. Many trustees—and, I am afraid, some administrators—persist in regarding faculty members as "personnel" to be hired and fired at the discretion of the management, just as some professors recognize no obligation to their college beyond the kind of formal responsibilities that are defined in a "union contract."

It seems to me that so long as these defects exist the academic profession is something less than professional. I should like to see AAUP—in cooperation with organizations representative of the colleges—bending more of their efforts to the development of a genuine professional spirit. Meanwhile, whether we like it or not, most faculties are likely to want the protection of a published policy on tenure.

In publicly supported institutions, especially, a written tenure policy, officially adopted and published, may be helpful in resisting external pressures. A strong president may need no such crutch when pressure is brought to bear to muzzle or get rid of a professor who espouses social, political or economic policies that are legitimate but unpopular, but if violent passions are aroused, the president may need all the help he can get. If I am not mistaken, assaults of this kind on the freedom of expression of certain scholars in public institutions gave the main impetus to the demand for published tenure policies. It has been chiefly in the large, publicly supported institutions that the greatest struggles for this essential freedom have occurred.

Even in a small college, however, the faculty may need some insurance, both against external pressures and against arbitrary actions on the part of the governing board or the administration, rare as the occasions may be for invoking it. In fairness it should be remembered that trustees and administrators have no monopoly on unreasonableness, and that a college has little effective recourse against a professor who proves negligent, cantankerous or antisocial, once he has safely passed the hurdle of probation. With or without a published tenure policy, the burden of proof will tend to lie on the administration, and this is as it should be. What is essential is that no faculty member should be penalized without due process. This can usually be assured without elaborate rules and procedures: a very simple statement of intent may well be sufficient.

You will see from all this that I do not think there is a compelling case for a published tenure policy in a college like yours. Assuming, however, that there is strong sentiment on the part of an important segment of your faculty for a published statement on tenure policy, you will of course wish to present some recommendation to your board of trustees. Depending on your own careful assessment of the situation, you might make one of the following proposals:

1. "The time is not opportune to publish a tenure policy. The record shows that the college has been eminently fair and just in all relationships with its faculty. The publication of a tenure policy at this time would seem to cast doubt on these dealings in the past and indicate distrust of the board of trustees and administration of the college."

2. "The college, through its board of trustees, accepts in general the principles enunciated in the joint statement on academic freedom and tenure adopted by the Association of American Colleges and the American Association of University Professors in 1940-41."

This proposal accepts the spirit and general principles of the "joint statement" but does not necessarily bind in all details.

3. Perhaps you think a more specific statement ought to be made, spelling out details. In that event, you can take the AAC-AAUP statement as your model and adapt it to your own particular situation. It would not be difficult, I think, to get samples of such adapted statements from other colleges.

Before you publish a tenure policy it would be well to make sure that you have a well-defined policy for terminating appointments. This is an area where there ought to be complete reciprocity between college and faculty member. That is, there should be frankness and consideration by the college for the faculty member and by the faculty member for the college.

It is obvious that *any* appointment, no matter what its terms, can be terminated by mutual agreement at any time. For other details on termination of appointments, I can do no better than refer you to the joint statements issued by the Association of American Colleges and the American Association of University Professors. These statements deal, in detail, with the distinction between term or probationary appointments and continuous appointments, and with procedures for the termination "for cause of a continuous appointment" and the dismissal "for cause of a teacher previous to the expiration of a term appointment." It is to be hoped that you will rarely, if ever, have need to invoke such procedures. Nevertheless, it is well to have established procedures on the books should the necessity ever arise.

There is another type of termination of appointment that should be mentioned: retirement for age. Most colleges have fixed an effective, often compulsory, retirement age. The age specified by action of the trustees varies considerably from college to college. It is seldom lower than sixty-five. The conditions governing retirement also vary. Sometimes retirement may be optional after a specified age and compulsory at a specified later date. When sixty-five is the specified retirement age, some colleges provide that one-year, or one-term, or part-time appointments may be granted in individual cases at the discretion of the president and the governing board.

There is, no doubt, something arbitrary about compulsory retirement. Nevertheless, in the long run it is in the best interests of all concerned—teacher, student and college. Without an automatic or compulsory requirement, each case has to be decided on an individual basis. In some cases this inevitably involves protest and heartache and often bitterness.

It must be said emphatically, however, that no college should have a retirement for age requirement unless it also has a funded retirement program in addition to Federal Social Security (OASI) coverage. Probably the best known and most widely used plan is that provided by the Teachers Insurance and Annuity Association. This non-profit agency was founded especially to assist colleges and universities in providing funded-income retirement programs for faculty members. The association also offers group insurance programs, notably in the field of major medical expense coverage and disability benefits. If you need further information, the association offices are always responsive to requests.

If I can be of further help in these matters, or in any other way, please call on me.

Sincerely,

# 10

## Academic Freedom

DEAR PRESIDENT MURDOCH:

I am very sorry to hear of the problem that Professor Stubby has created. His advocacy of "free love" in his sociology class precipitates for you the whole issue of academic freedom.

There is not the slightest doubt in my mind that you are justified in taking a strong stand against him. His personal conviction of the "soundness of free love" gives him no right to take advantage of his position as a teacher to propagate his unorthodox opinions in the classroom. What he advocates is against all your college stands for as well as being opposed to our civil code. If he does not heed your warning you have no other choice than to institute proceedings to effect his dismissal from the college. His claim that you are denying him academic freedom should not deter you in the least.

Part of the reason for such happenings is confusion about the meaning of academic freedom. Many of the statements we see are so vague that they are open to almost any interpretation. Let me illustrate. One writer in an educational journal defined academic freedom as "the right to be honest in thought, in utterance and behavior." This statement has the virtue of being brief and positive, but it is so vague and general as to be of no practical value. It is less open to misinterpretation, however, than another and contrasting statement which appeared some time later in the same journal.

Here, at greater length, academic freedom was defined as

"the absence of, or protection from, such restraints or pressures —chiefly in the form of sanctions threatened by state or church authorities or by the authorities, faculties or students of colleges and universities, but occasionally also by other power groups in society—as are designed to create in the minds of scholars fears and anxieties that may inhibit them from freely studying and investigating whatever they are interested in, and from freely discussing, teaching or publishing whatever opinions they have reached."

This definition, I submit, is the kind that invites trouble. It is statements like this that give comfort to men like Professor Stubby—perhaps the one teacher out of a hundred or more who would try to read into such statements justification for their anti-social attitudes.

I believe we are on safe ground, however, with the joint statement of the Association of American Colleges and the American Association of University Professors on academic freedom and tenure. As you read that statement, you will find that there are proper cautions for the college and university teacher. He is urged to remember that, when he speaks or writes as a citizen, "the public may judge his profession and his institution by his utterances. Hence he should at all times be accurate, should exercise appropriate restraint, should show respect for the opinions of others." Again, when he is dealing with controversial matters, he is warned to make it clear that he speaks or writes "not as an institutional spokesman" but only in his capacity as a private citizen.

This is certainly reasonable enough. No wise president, no understanding governing board, will wish to deny a professor's right, *as a citizen,* to take a stand on any controversial issue. But there are canons of propriety and restraint which the professor himself should have in mind and should observe; and presidents and governing boards have a right to expect such a sense of institutional responsibility on the part of faculty members.

The statement is no less reasonable on the subject of the teacher in the classroom. While it declares that the teacher is entitled to freedom in discussing his subject, he is cautioned to "be careful not to introduce into his teaching controversial matter which has no relation to his subject."

The joint statement also makes clear that there may be some legitimate limitation of academic freedom in certain institutions by reason of their special purpose or character. Thus a church-related college, because of its religious objectives, may require certain limitations that would not apply to a state university. In such instances, "limitations of academic freedom because of religious or other aims of the institution should be clearly stated in writing at the time of the appointment."

On its side, of course, the college or the university must recognize that "Academic freedom in its teaching aspect is fundamental for the protection of the rights of the teacher in teaching and of the student to freedom in learning." Also the college must recognize that a faculty member does not give up his rights as a citizen, and that when he speaks or writes as a citizen he should be free from institutional prescription, provided that he makes it clear that he does not speak or write as a representative of the institution.

Do not be concerned about the threat of Dr. Stubby to appeal his case to the American Association of University Professors. Although, of course, I cannot speak for AAUP, I doubt they would give your professor any support in this instance. It might, however, be useful for you to discuss the case in person with officers of the association in Washington in advance of any investigation. Some colleges have found this helpful as a means of reaching amicable understanding and avoiding fuss and bother that would not be good for either party. I believe that the AAUP files hold records of many such cases to which no publicity was ever given.

I can understand your impatience with AAUP and what you term their "overconcern" with academic freedom. But in fairness it must be said that there are some famous instances on record where academic people have suffered greatly from outside pressure groups who wanted them silenced or dismissed for upholding truths that were opposed by these groups or were unpopular at the time. On this score at least, AAUP deserves credit for alerting the educational world to serious dangers.

These dangers have appeared lately in regard to unpopular views on race relations and there may well be other evidence in the future in the wake of such movements as the John Birch Society.

I find no difficulty in agreeing with most, if not all, of the statements on academic freedom issued by AAUP. But the fundamental principles are easy enough to state: the real problem is to apply them in a given situation.

Sometimes I think it is unfortunate that the phrase "academic freedom" was ever coined. It appears to set this freedom apart as a kind of super-freedom exempt from the reasonable limitations that qualify the exercise of other types of freedom. On the contrary, it seems to me, academic freedom is only one aspect of the intellectual and spiritual climate that characterizes a healthy, democratic society. This particular aspect is singled out for special emphasis only because the academic institution cannot perform its distinctive role except in a climate of freedom.

The desire for freedom is innate because the Creator endowed man with freedom of the will, which exempts him from any absolute necessity in choice or in action. But this priceless gift brings with it the great responsibility to see that neither the rights of God nor of other men are harmed thereby. Since man is not an isolated being, there is at least a moral necessity to limit his freedom. Academic freedom is subject to the same limitations as the other freedoms that free men possess: it cannot be absolute in the strict sense of the word.

There is no doubt that the great majority of American citizens are passionately devoted to the freedoms which we enjoy. No sensible American would wish this country to fall under a communist or fascist dictatorship. But observe the wide differences in conceptions of what is necessary to preserve our freedoms. On the one hand you have those who advocate that this country arm to the teeth and then beat the threatening aggressor to the punch by annihilating him before he can attack. At the other extreme you have those who believe that the only way to peace and the preservation of our freedom is through unilateral disarmament and the destruction of our stockpiles of nuclear weapons. Those who try to advocate a more reasonable middle course are subject to criticism from both extremes.

It seems to me that there is a close parallel to this situation in the academic world. On the one side we have AAUP and the American Civil Liberties Union, which sometimes seem to advocate freedom at any price. On the other side we have the parents of our students, who fear the subversion or corruption of their youth, and we have our benefactors and the general public, who may be influenced by more or less selfish motives. It is not always easy to follow the sane middle course.

Usually we take it for granted that one who freely accepts appointment to the staff of a definitely church-related college has the prudence and courtesy not to attack or go contrary to the ideals for which the college stands. But your experience with Dr. Stubby should make it evident that you can not assume this in all cases.

Perhaps your greatest weakness was the absence of anything in your teaching agreement, in your faculty handbook or in your catalogue that makes any reference either to academic freedom or to any limitations on that freedom.

As a safeguard for the future, why not incorporate in your teaching agreement, faculty handbook and catalogue some such brief statement as the following:

Members of the faculty enjoy full freedom to pursue the truth and to teach the truth as they see it, but they are not free, of course, to advocate doctrines subversive of American constitutional government and political liberties or of the aims and purposes of this college, a church-related institution committed to the upholding of Christian faith and morality.

Out of your present unhappy experience can come at least this provision for the future. Meanwhile I trust that you will see your present problem to a conclusion without further embarrassment.

Sincerely,

# 11

## Administrative Organization
## of the Faculty

Dear President Smythe:

It was not wholly unexpected that, in reply to my remark about reducing the number of academic departments, you should in turn ask me how one can effect such a reduction. As a matter of fact, I had thought about being more explicit but feared it would make my letter too long and involved. I think the question can be treated adequately in this letter.

Almost invariably I have found that in the college of moderate size the faculty is greatly overorganized. I think the difficulty has been that relatively small colleges are too uncritical in copying details of university organization.

A college or university with faculty members numbered in the hundreds must, for efficient operation, divide and even subdivide. As a consequence, the large institutions have schools, divisions and departments with a quota of vice-presidents, deans, directors and chairmen. In a sense, all of these operational units perpetually challenge the unity of the university. Probably the departmental system has been the most troublesome, because each subject-matter field tends to become a separate entity. Each department has its own chairman, holds its own meetings, submits its own budget, seeks representation on this or that university committee, and so on.

Up to a point this is good, but it can lead to a shortsighted departmental rivalry that results in efforts at aggrandizement, a spirit of snobbery and a departmentalized education. Valiant efforts have been made by universities to control these divagations, which are not intended but just grow like Topsy. Projects for cooperation have been proposed and implemented. But even the very important and currently popular area studies have not succeeded in dispelling the insularity of the departmental system. Nor have the various types of interdepartmental survey or general education courses been wholly successful.

Now the college which numbers its full-time faculty with two digits has no need for all the divisions and subdivisions of a university. On the contrary, it is desirable to have as few of these units as may be consistent with efficient operation. Many small colleges, however, have patterned their organizational structure on the university and have taken over its terminology without considering whether or not such a structure is practicable. As a consequence, some colleges have almost as many departments as there are subject-matter fields, each with a designated chairman.

Sometimes a divisional arrangement will be superimposed on these departments, with still further chairmen. This merely complicates matters. If its purpose is to break down departmental barriers, the added divisional arrangement serves instead to set up new barriers. If it is done for administrative purposes, as the appointment of chairmen would seem to indicate, the added divisions involve more complicated procedures. Divisional grouping of subject-matter fields may be quite useful for curriculum arrangement, but it can serve no purpose administratively unless it completely *replaces* departmental organization.

The overorganization of such colleges is immediately apparent if one takes the catalogue of a college and checks the number of faculty members against the various divisions, departments and standing committees. Some curious situations have come to light in this way. For example, there was one college with a faculty of fifty-four members which had twenty-two chairmen of divisions and departments and twenty-two chairmen of various standing committees. This made a total of forty-four chairmen out of the faculty of fifty-four! At another college, one faculty member was chairman of both a division and a department and another was chairman of two departments and held membership in a third. The college with a department for every one-and-a-half faculty members may be an extreme instance, but the trend is definitely present in many colleges.

Every college needs some type of faculty organization designed to suit the needs and size of the college. A reasonable number of functional units based on some community of interests seems to be indicated. No fixed number can be arbitrarily prescribed. Both the number and the composition of these faculty units may differ from college to college. Each college must decide for itself the number of functional units that it can justify, based upon an analysis of its faculty.

Perhaps the simplest way to make this analysis is to list on separate index cards the various subject-matter fields or departments in which courses are now offered—English, history, mathematics, philosophy, and so forth. On each card, list the full-time and part-time teachers in the respective fields, with the proviso that no person may be listed on more than one card.

With the cards spread out before one, it should then be possible to see at a glance numerical strengths and weaknesses on a departmental or subject-matter basis. The chances are that, out of eighteen or more subject-matter areas, many will be found not to warrant departmental status, simply because there are not enough teachers to constitute a group that can meet together and accept departmental responsibilities. It is possible, however, to reconstitute the faculty organization so as to have five, six or seven functional units. With due regard for community of interests, subject-matter fields can be combined in thoroughly defensible departments that will have the numerical strength necessary for functional units.

Some combinations are clearly logical and can be readily determined. Thus it would be unrealistic today to recognize any academic barriers between the physical sciences and mathematics; between languages, ancient and modern; among the fine arts; or among the social studies. Other combinations, like education, library science, home economics and so on, would have to be rationalized a bit in order to group them together under some such title as the "Department of Service Arts." But it has been done.

"Now all this is very fine," I hear you say, "but how does one 'sell' it to the faculty?" Well, I admit, there can be a bit of a problem here—but it is not insoluble. In my visits to colleges I have never found a proposal for streamlining the faculty organization running into objections from presidents, deans or registrars. Quite the contrary! But I have met some sharp opposition from faculty members (perhaps deposable chairmen) and have debated this with them in open meeting, with some success. If you run into any difficulty with your faculty I would be glad to debate the matter with them. Sometimes an outsider can be more convincing because of his detachment.

Before meeting with faculty groups to propose and discuss a reduction in the number of academic departments, I have followed a uniform procedure in all the colleges where this issue has been raised. In the first place the whole problem has been discussed in depth with the dean. Together we have analyzed the faculty structure with its numerical strengths and weaknesses. We have then reconstructed the faculty organization as we thought most practicable in the light of all the circumstances. Having arrived at an agreement in our own minds, we have discussed the matter with the president to get the benefit of his views.

In meeting with the faculty, therefore, I am usually well informed on the local situation, sometimes even forewarned as to where opposition can be expected. As an outsider I have no entanglements, nothing to lose or gain personally, so that I can be objective and frank. In some cases a mere recital of the details of the present faculty organization brings a laugh of surprise from the audience. When you have a situation with a number of one-man or less-than-one-man departments—even two-men departments—with two out of every three faculty members listed as chairmen of divisions, departments or standing committees, the evident absurdities predispose the faculty to recognize that reorganization is necessary.

It is then possible to advert to the trend toward self-study and self-evaluation among colleges and universities; to the need for re-examining old ideas and old ways of doing things, so as to bring up to date whatever may have lagged behind; to the necessity of increasing the efficiency of internal organization in order to achieve more effective operation and to meet the criticisms of businessmen, who are now expected to contribute liberally to the promotion of higher education.

In suggesting combinations of subject-matter fields to make defensible departments, it is important to give the reasons that require such combinations. One can point, for example, to the developments that have brought the physical sciences and mathematics closer together; to the common use of expensive equipment, computer centers, and laboratories for radioactive materials; to current researches in linguistics, language laboratories and so on.

It is important to allay some of the fears that may arise. Grouping subject-matter fields in one department does not denote a consolidation or merger of courses, desirable as this might be in some instances. It does not subordinate any of the fields of learning, nor does it mean that one discipline shall dominate over another. It need have no effect on the majors or minors that are being offered. If there is proliferation of courses and majors, this is a distinct problem which must be solved independently.

From the administrative point of view, the advantages of reorganizing the faculty are so obvious that a brief mention of some of them should be sufficient.

Reorganization along the lines indicated will of course eliminate the one-man, two-men and three-men departments and provide functional units to which definite responsibilities can be assigned. It will be easier to find among the faculty five, six or seven effective department chairmen than eighteen or twenty. It will be easier to insist on regular departmental meetings and the preparation and circulation of adequate minutes. It will be easier for the dean to be in regular communication with five, six or seven chairmen than with three times as many.

At the same time, the functioning of these departments will

help to relieve the dean of an inordinate burden of details. In some instances, at least, it will greatly assist the business office in both budget preparation and control. Finally, this broader concept of membership in a department necessarily brings closer together members of various disciplines. It will therefore facilitate that wider interdisciplinary understanding and collaboration which, although earnestly desired, is so difficult to attain in the larger university.

The success of the new departmental arrangement will depend largely upon the administrative ability of the chairmen selected. It would seem important, therefore, to avoid anything that might give rise to the impression that a chairmanship is a kind of super-rank with implied tenure and vested rights. It would be well to have it understood that the chairmanship of a department is not dependent on rank, seniority, degrees or any other criteria than the ability to do the work required of the position. Probably appointments should be made by the president yearly or for some other definite and reasonably short term of service. Reappointment should be possible—but not obligatory—after completion of the term. If it is considered practicable, there could be some kind of rotation for chairmen. In any event, a change of chairmen need imply no disparagement of the incumbent.

If I can be of further assistance, please let me know. Meanwhile, be assured that I shall be interested to know the outcome of your efforts.

Sincerely,

# 12

## Preparing the Ground
## for a New Curriculum

DEAR DR. WILLIFORD:

The meetings with your committee on curriculum during my recent visit were most interesting and stimulating. Although I have been engaged in administration for a good many years, I have never lost interest in the basic issues involved in the organization of a college curriculum, and in these college visits nothing gives me greater satisfaction than to join in such lively discussion as took place during my sessions with your committee.

In this letter I want to make some general observations on the background against which the restudy of your curriculum is taking place and on the procedures you are following. Later, if you think it will be helpful, I shall be glad to comment on some of the details which the curriculum committee and then the faculty as a whole will have under consideration.

There seems to be quite general agreement on the purposes and goals of Woodbury as an institution of higher learning. This does not preclude disagreement and vigorous debate on details, but it does happily eliminate the danger of persistent splits on fundamental issues. Your statement of aims, now approved by faculty and trustees, is one of the better ones among the many I have seen. In any such brief statement it is virtually impossible to escape a certain idealistic vagueness and the appearance of aspiring to the unattainable. But this doesn't trouble me now as much as it once did. The real test comes in the working out in practice of the implications of the professed ideals. The revision of your curriculum will be a part of this process.

It is quite clear that your plans for the future have been carefully made and that in this planning you have had the cooperation of trustees, administrative officers and faculty. You anticipate some increase in enrollment, but you expect it to come gradually, under careful control. You have made realistic projections of your needs for additional faculty and facilities. Thus you are able to relate your curricular revision to potential enrollments and possible income. You are wisely proposing to keep these plans flexible and subject to modification as conditions change. Long-range planning is highly advisable, even essential, provided that plans are not thought of as so final and binding that adjustments cannot be made. You are fully aware that the making of a plan is not an end but only a beginning. No plan will execute itself. There must be vision, enthusiasm, persistence and teamwork on the part of all those who share responsibility with you.

I know that there are some fairly radical changes you wish to make and that some of them may involve departure from well-established practices and perhaps a threat to vested interests. You are very wise not to try to impose your ideas on the faculty or to hurry the process of change. A faculty may be submissive. It may be openly rebellious. It is much better if changes are made after free discussion, understanding, and the achievement of consensus, even if this involves a certain amount of compromise. Even with the kind of basic agreements that have been reached by your faculty, there may still be wide variations of judgment on specific questions.

Another thing is quite clear: Woodbury is definitely committed to the ideals of liberal education. The nature of liberal education and its relationships to other types of education and training will continue for a long time, I am sure, to be subjects of debate and experimentation. The questions at issue have to do with the basic problems of education in a democracy. There is and will continue to be room for a great variety of institutions of education beyond the high school in the pattern of American education. In fact, as you well know, this variety is often cited as one of the strengths of the American pattern, though one may sometimes think that confusion and chaos are more apt terms.

Liberal education is sometimes interpreted by its critics as implying subservience to an outworn tradition. It means for these critics a lifeless, routine performance by students of meaningless and irrelevant tasks imposed by a teacher who is interested only in his *subject* and has little concern for *students*. This, I suggest, and I think you will agree, is a distortion.

Liberal education can be and should be vital, stimulating, exciting, relevant. But relevance cannot properly mean relationship only to the contemporary, to the immediate, to the current needs of the student as he apprehends them. Liberal education seeks relevance to *long-range* needs which the maturing young person, because of his very immaturity, cannot wholly foresee. The liberal arts college seeks to give the student resources for dealing with the unexpected, the unforeseen, the unforeseeable. It seeks also to arouse and to cultivate interests that will make for continuing growth as a person, for broadening horizons and deeper insights. Inspiration, excitement, involvement in current problems, whether local or worldwide, can be a part of getting a liberal education. They cannot be the whole of it. Hard work, perhaps not in itself interesting; the doing of imposed tasks, because they are essential to mastery of a subject or technique; the persistent effort to understand and to think—these are requirements which demand often the privacy of the library and the study.

Certainly during the four college years the vocational and professional interests of young people cannot and should not be ignored. But we can insist on concern for the *person* as well as for his vocational competence and his adjustment to his environment as it now is. When this concern for enrichment of the resources of the person is subordinated to or overshadowed by the narrowly vocational or professional, or even by concern for the solution of contemporary problems, the liberal, or liberating, function of education is being discounted.

I have found quite distressing, in some of the colleges I have come to know, the contrast between what they profess and what they practice. While avowing devotion to the ideals of liberal education, they include much in their curricula that seems to me to have no claim to such recognition. I know that some of this is due to the necessity such colleges were under to attract students in the desperate struggle for survival during the pre-war and wartime years. It is to be hoped that such necessity is disappearing and that every college can choose its courses freely and then honestly conform practice to profession, whatever the choice and whatever the profession. I am very sure that a dominant concern for liberal education means the exclusion from the curriculum of anything that cannot justify itself in terms of intellectual challenge or its contribution to richness and resource of personality. This is not to deny the value of some of the excluded things. They simply do not contribute to the purposes of *liberal education.*

I must mention one thing that to me is gratifying. You and your faculty are accepting the preparation of teachers as a responsibility of the college, and of the whole faculty of the college. You recognize this as a responsibility that in no way conflicts with the aims of the liberal arts program. A good many of your subject-matter faculty people are vitally interested and are joining actively in your planning in this area.

I know, of course, that there are difficulties, some of them resulting from certification and accreditation requirements. These difficulties are the common lot of American colleges, and the issues have for some years been vigorously debated on national and regional levels. What seems to me unfortunate is the antagonism, which has at times been so acute, between the "educationists" and the "subject-matter" specialists. Granting the extremes to which the emphasis on "method" has gone, it is also true, I think, that the liberal arts devotees have sometimes virtually abdicated their responsibility and lost an opportunity that they should have retained. Every indication of a lessening of this antagonism and of a willingness to cooperate in a vitally important service is most encouraging.

I am quite sure that there is now and will continue to be need for the type of college Woodbury proposes to be. There is, of course, no one pattern of curriculum, no one educational procedure that alone can serve the purposes of liberal education. Your committee will, I am sure, be studying carefully the curricula of other colleges. But you will need to copy no one. You can achieve excellence within your own terms of reference. The college that is willing to remain relatively small, to limit its program to the requirements of a clearly defined purpose, and to devote its resources to the highest possible achievement within the defined limits can render essential and even distinguished service. You and your faculty will, I am confident, work out an educational program that is authentically yours and that will admirably serve your students and your constituency.

It occurs to me now, in concluding this letter, to say that of course no curriculum, however carefully worked out on paper, is any good without good teaching. This does not mean for me, however, that the curriculum is unimportant. I think that what is taught has significance. A truly great teacher can, it is said, make any subject so vital and stimulating as to broaden horizons and stretch minds. But William Rainey Harpers teaching Hebrew are exceedingly rare. *Good* teachers are, I venture to say, more numerous than is sometimes granted. Most of us, I suspect, can remember and feel grateful to more than an occasional teacher who has helped us—though his bibliography is limited or non-existent; though he appears in no directory of scholars; even though his name would be recognized only by those who learned from him the meaning of scholarship and caught from him some of the zest of intellectual adventure. I could name such men, and so could you.

Who is a good teacher? What is good teaching? Well, after all my years of experience, I have no pat answers, no yardsticks, no formulae. In any case, such questions must be put aside for another time and, I think, for some one else to answer.

I shall be happy to hear from you and to write further if there is occasion to do so. I am greatly interested in the progress of your committee's work. Please keep me informed.

Sincerely,

# 13

## Guide Lines for Planning
## the Curriculum

DEAR DR. WILLIFORD:

Our letters evidently crossed in the mail. I think in my letter
I anticipated and commented on some of the questions you
raise. You ask, however, for some specific suggestions on curricular organization. You ask also for some further explanation
of my insistence, in the discussion with your committee, on the
responsibility of the *whole* faculty for the *whole* college curriculum. Some members of the committee, you indicate, are
somewhat apprehensive of intrusion on strictly departmental
or individual responsibility. I comment on this latter item first.

I think my emphasis on this point was largely due to the fact
that I have encountered curricula whose organization indicated
that the faculty had almost completely abdicated responsibility
in relation to the total educational program. Departments and
divisions seemed pretty much to go their own way in almost
complete independence. Sometimes it has been difficult to
discover the curriculum *of the college.* Divisional and pre-
vocational and pre-professional programs were laid out in me-
ticulous detail, but one had to "tease out" laboriously the common elements. Further, a student had to identify himself with
a department or a division or one of these special programs
from the time of his first registration as a freshman. This seems

to me a great mistake, even when there is ample provision for change later on.

It is my conviction that the faculty as a whole should be responsible for and have authority over the curriculum as a whole. This implies a special responsibility for courses that are required of all candidates for a degree: responsibility for the requirement and for the nature and content of the courses themselves. A somewhat more limited, but nonetheless real, responsibility rests on the whole faculty for *all* courses accepted for degree credit. Any new course to be offered should be approved by the faculty or by a duly authorized and representative committee of the faculty. A student's entire program should be subject to approval by a properly designated adviser and to review by the dean.

I do not mean, of course, that the entire faculty should examine every detail of every course. Professors and departments can be trusted—and have to be—for most of what is included in the courses offered. But general understanding on the part of the faculty is most desirable, I think, and any professor or department head should be ready and willing to interpret and, in broad terms, to justify any course, especially a new course proposed for inclusion in the curriculum. I shall want to suggest, later on, one or two other points on which the authority of the whole faculty should, in my judgment, be recognized.

Now to get at some of the other questions touched on in our discussions and correspondence, I make certain assumptions as to the general structure of the curriculum. A faculty must recognize, for example, that *selection* is inevitable, since not everything that might be thought desirable can be included in the curriculum or in the basic requirements. Furthermore, some subjects are more important than others. Here there is obviously occasion for almost endless debate. In the end, in the shaping of a curriculum there must in all likelihood be some measure of compromise, some yielding of personal predilections and of departmental interests.

I assume also that there will be a reasonable balance or proportionate division among: courses required of all candidates for a degree; courses required for a major or for specialization in a chosen field; courses grouped together, from which, for purposes of distribution, a student may choose a specified number, i.e., optional courses or restricted electives; and free electives.

There will be, of course, a distinction between introductory and advanced courses. This is virtually universal practice. But one question suggests itself: introductory to what? or, perhaps better, introductory for whom? Should the introductory courses be thought of as preparation for advanced courses and therefore be designed for the prospective or potential specialist? Or should they be so designed as to provide the kind of acquaintance with a field of intellectual interest that any well-educated person should have? Should the college curriculum provide two different types of introductory courses? Or can both purposes be achieved in the same introductory course? On the one hand, there will be heard warnings against superficiality. On the other hand, there will be protests against the overly technical and against failure even to suggest the broad human values and the relationships of the subject matter.

I'd love to hear your committee, and your faculty as a whole, bat such questions around. Just stating them is as far as I now want to go.

There will, I am sure, be specifications as to which of the required and optional courses must be taken during the first two years. Just how much of the block of required and group-option courses should be specified for completion during the first two years will depend on how many such courses there are and on just how much freedom of choice the group options allow the student.

My own experience, supplemented by observation, suggests the undesirability of making the requirements for the first two years too rigid. I think there should be provision, aside from the group options, for some free choice on the part of the student—some really free election even for the underclassman. Just how much in terms of a percentage I am not prepared to say. Of course I do not question the desirability of certain basic uniform requirements to be met during the first two years, supplemented by options within carefully devised groups of subjects or courses. But I do question the advisability and the practicability of having such requirements constitute the whole of the freshman and sophomore curriculum.

In the provision of options or restricted electives for students, subjects or specific courses are grouped together, and a specified number of courses must be taken from each group. The groupings often correspond to recognized divisions of scholarship, e.g., the humanities, the social studies, the natural sciences. Such groupings can be made without the necessity of setting up divisions as administrative units, with a chairman for each. I am not here concerned with the organization of the faculty for administrative purposes but with the grouping of the subjects for curricular purposes. Even so, such groupings vary widely, and problems arise as to the placing of some subjects, for example, history and psychology.

I assume that, under your new curricular plan, you will expect each student, at least by his junior year, to have chosen a major or field of specialization. This choice will in large measure determine his program of studies during his last two college years. Here I have this concern: Surely the faculty, or a duly authorized committee, must approve the offering of a major by a department or a division. But this is not enough. The department or the division thus approved should not be completely free to fix requirements for the major in terms of number of courses, number of hours, or specific courses. An occasional department may wish to require too little. It is much more likely that some departments will want to require too much. By so doing they ignore or deny the continued importance, on this relatively advanced level of college experience, of breadth of interest and of some freedom of choice for the student. Hence the suggestion that the faculty as a whole set both lower *and* upper limits to the requirements for a major.

Now another point of concern. I am assuming, obviously, that the uniform required courses, the group-option courses, and the courses required for the major will not have filled up the individual student's entire program, and that there will therefore be fairly generous room for some free electives during the junior and senior years. I think that to some extent the choice of these electives should be controlled. I do not myself like the device of requiring a minor or minors in addition to the major. Greater flexibility is provided by some kind of distribution requirement, i.e., a requirement that a certain proportion of these electives be taken outside the major department, even outside related departments. For example, the science major should have some work in social studies and some in humanistic studies—yes, I would say right through the senior year.

I add here the suggestion that there should also be for the upperclassman at least a minimum of completely free choice. Then I go one step further and suggest that the junior or the senior should be allowed to take some elementary or introductory courses by way of sampling some field of interest with which he has had no contact. Of course I would not want the senior to be in position just to pick at random, according to convenience of schedule or the reputation of a course as "easy." But this may be his last chance to get some acquaintance with an important area of intellectual interest. I have known of some instances in which such delayed contact has completely redirected a student's life. The faculty, or an individual instructor, may wish to impose some additional requirements on a junior or a senior taking a course offered primarily for underclassmen. Or departments may find it desirable to design introductory courses especially for upperclassmen. My concern is only that such last-chance access not be denied the student who seriously wants it.

I need hardly record my conviction that going to college should not be just a matter of passing a specified number of courses according to a prescribed pattern. Certainly by the final year of his college experience the student should have developed a more mature attitude and some real understanding of "what it is all about." Thus it should not be necessary— though for some it may be a wise precaution—to have regulations that prevent overconcentration on the one hand or aimless and uncoordinated choice of electives on the other. This, however, is a negative provision. Positively, every effort should be made to insure that the work of the senior year becomes a maturing and synthesizing experience for the student.

Specially planned senior courses and seminars; senior essays; various types of comprehensive examinations, either in the student's major field or more general in character, such as the Graduate Record Examination—these are among the plans that have been used to serve the purposes I am suggesting. Your committee members will, I am sure, wish to familiarize themselves with the experience of other colleges in using such plans.

The curricular revision you now have under way at Woodbury gives you opportunity to tackle the virtually universal problem of overproliferation of courses. The pruning that will take place may cause some pain but will, I am sure, be salutary. But a word of warning: it will probably need to be done all over again in a very few years. In any case, however, there is no reason to fear that your curriculum will ever exhibit the kind of absurdities that are sometimes encountered; for example, a one-man department listing more courses than appear in the Yale catalogue.

One other item on which there is great variation: the naming of degrees. I have only this suggestion: Don't multiply the number of different degrees you offer. Keep the degree scheme simple, *but,* make each degree mean something. I think this can be done. Often it isn't.

I am sure we could talk at length about each of these items, and there is much more I'd enjoy talking with you about. Please let me know if there are other questions on which you might wish me to comment in writing.

Sincerely,

# 14

## Some Special Features of Curricular Planning

DEAR DR. WILLIFORD:

It is gratifying to know that you and Dean Barton found my recent letters interesting and that you have shared them with the members of your committee on curriculum. Now, at the instance of the committee, you suggest several specific questions which are under consideration, and discussion of which may be helpful. Since I cannot at any time soon schedule another visit, I must write about these questions. I continue, however, to hope that we may have a chance later for some face-to-face discussion. I very much enjoy the kind of give and take made possible by such discussion. Misunderstandings can be cleared up, and any seeming dogmatism can be avoided as it cannot in writing. On some of the questions you raise I have fairly strong opinions, but assuredly I do not wish to be dogmatic.

You mention first the question of interdepartmental general education courses. The term "general education" itself raises some questions, of course. I assume that your committee is using the term in the context of a liberal arts program. To begin with, let me say that I think it unfortunate that in the minds of a good many faculty people general education has come to be identified exclusively with the interdepartmental type of course organization. Such courses seem still to have appeal. But there are often serious difficulties in their planning and staffing. They have been far from uniformly successful. And I have come to believe quite definitely that in most colleges the aims of general education, liberally interpreted, can be served most effectively through proper coordination of departmental courses.

I recall one college which, after long experience with general education courses of the interdepartmental or transdepartmental type, had made a remarkably thorough, honest, objective evaluation of these courses. Probably the most significant comment in the whole voluminous report was one to the effect that, after all these years, the general education courses were not so well organized nor so effective as most of the departmentally based courses. Note was taken, also, of student complaints that there was quite a lot of overlapping or duplication, even to the use of the same books for required reading in the humanities and the social studies courses.

Incidentally, this college had been so thoroughly committed to this type of curricular organization that some of the departments not directly related to the general education courses had almost died of neglect. For example, there was no degree requirement in foreign language or in mathematics, and provisions for these fields were meager.

One single instance cannot, of course, discredit the whole concept of such course organization. The fault may have been wholly local. But this instance does at least suggest some of the hazards.

Your second question has to do with special provisions for the superior or able student, and special honors courses. Certainly I approve of the idea of such planning. I venture to suggest, first, that such programs and courses should not involve simply requiring more of the same. I have encountered this type of honors course. Special programs should be different in quality and in challenge. I suggest also that admission to them should not depend solely on high grades and high test scores. Motivation, special interest, ambition on the part of the less academically successful, demonstrated originality, independence, creativeness—these things, insofar as they can be identified, should be taken into account. I think I should be willing to admit to such courses *any* student who could convince me that he really wanted to try them.

Special plans for honors students often include provision for independent study. This phrase suggests an educational reform that has been widely and enthusiastically advocated. With the intent of this advocacy I am in thorough accord. I believe that students should more and more be encouraged to assume responsibility for their own education. But I have come to realize that there are hazards in provisions for independent study by undergraduates.

To be effective, such study requires careful guidance and supervision, frequent checking, and searching criticism of the results. Independent study cannot be thought of as simply a device for reducing the professor's teaching load or relieving the student of the necessity of attending classes. It actually makes heavy demands on the teacher's time, if it is properly done. Otherwise a student may be tempted just to "coast" until the deadline for a report or an essay is near; then he will work desperately to get something done. Even more serious is the fact that an earnest, industrious student may come up with something that shows an impressive amount of work, of hours put in, but which shows no real originality, even no real comprehension. This kind of thing has no educational value. It may do real harm. If your committee wants to provide for independent study, be sure they count the cost.

A third question, intensely interesting to me, relates to advanced placement, early admissions, and acceleration. I am glad your committee is giving consideration to the issues involved. We are all well aware of the common complaints about the ill-prepared student, the virtually illiterate high school graduate. We all regret the necessity, which so many colleges have faced, of providing remedial courses, for which degree credit has sometimes been allowed. Perhaps the day is not far distant when this necessity will disappear. But in the evolving relationships between high school and college a quite different type of question has attracted increasing attention—the question now raised by your committee.

I have long thought that there was too much overlapping,

duplication, repetition, in the work of the last two years of high school and the first two years of college, and I have at times spoken strongly on the subject. Such overlapping and repetition are particularly regrettable and harmful in their impact on the bright, academically superior student. Such an eager student often finds himself compelled in college to take courses covering the same ground he has already been over in high school: English composition, for example, or a survey of English literature, or history, or mathematics; elementary chemistry, biology, or physics. Examples of these and of other duplications can easily be found. The consequence, for the bright student, is all too apt to be loss of interest, the stifling of curiosity, often the actual encouragement of careless and slovenly habits of work.

What is needed, in my judgment, is much better coordination between the curriculum of the good high school—good, in this context, in terms of preparation for college—and the curriculum of the college. To this I would add provision for acceleration on the part of the student capable of it. I believe that, with such coordination and such provisions, one or two years can be saved for the really able student without any lowering of the level of attainment or any sacrifice of quality.

The provisions for acceleration may vary. For some it may mean admission to college before completion of the formal high school curriculum. It may mean advanced standing for the entering high school graduate—allowing college credit for work done in high school. It may mean allowing the college student to move ahead at a faster pace than the average, without having to "serve time" as fixed in the conventional academic calendar.

While in recent years there has been much interest in such proposals, college faculties are typically quite cautious and hesitant in their approach to them. It may be that the failure of the University of Chicago's drastic move in relocating the bachelor's degree has made us all wary. In any case, college faculties have been reluctant to allow any degree credit for work done in high school or anywhere else outside the college classroom. Experimental programs involving cooperation among selected high schools and colleges have usually put the emphasis upon enrichment; acceleration has been almost taboo. College fac-

ulties have been willing to grant exemption from specific requirements and to allow advanced placement in a given subject-
matter sequence, while refusing to allow actual degree credit
for demonstrated achievement and thus a reduction in the time
and in the number of courses required for attainment of a college degree.

I have found, it is fair to say, a surprising and to me a gratifying number of college faculties that now allow not only ex-
emptions and advanced placement in a given subject but actual
college credit as well. I am all for it. I am not afraid of acceleration for the student demonstrably capable of it. I must add,
however, that I am not endorsing hastily devised or carelessly
administered programs for the purposes under consideration.
More experience is necessary. Proper levels of attainment must
be ensured. Careful controls are necessary.

Your faculty, as would almost any faculty, will probably wish
to prescribe the methods by which a student can qualify for
early admission or for advanced standing or for acceleration in
his college work. To begin with, the faculty may wish to set
limits to the amount of advanced standing a student can be
allowed, or to the amount of work above the normal he may be
allowed to take in the interest of acceleration. It may very well
wish to require that a fairly large proportion of the work accepted for the degree be done at Woodbury. Certainly, in my
judgment, at least one year of work above the sophomore level
should be included in the minimum residence requirement—
preferably the senior year. This, I think, is justified on the
ground that the student on whom the college puts its stamp by
conferring a degree should have spent an effective period of
time under its tutelage. But I hope the restrictions will not be
too rigid and that the approach of your faculty will not be too
hesitant.

I know that there are limits, and that there are real dangers
in acceleration under external pressures. It may be noted, incidentally, that such pressures can be dangerous also for less
able students whose parents or friends put pressure on them
when they fail to make good grades. In spite of the risks, however, I do not think we are justified in subjecting the capable,

interested, eager student to boredom, making him kill time and delaying too long his attainment of that level of intellectual achievement of which he is capable. We may ruin him in the process.

I cannot refrain from adding the suggestion that some of the proposals under discussion in this letter may have relevance to a type of student to whom, I often think, we give too little thought. We have always given much time and attention to the student who is failing or about to fail. We have always been able to identify and in some way give recognition to the student who consistently makes high grades: now we are greatly concerned to find ways of making special provision for his superior abilities. But it seems to me that we have given little special thought to those students who are with us in much larger numbers.

They constitute no problem, at least academically. They seem to be content with respectable passing grades. Many of them make such grades with little difficulty. They may not be academically minded. Certainly they are not exactly scholarly in their tastes. There is in their make-up nothing of the pedantic, as there sometimes is in the grade-making, if not grade-hunting, student. They may be bored by the routine of the classroom; it fails to take hold of them. They devote their energies and their real abilities to extracurricular activities; often they become student leaders. Often, too, they become, later on, highly successful business or professional men whom we put on our boards of trustees and to whom we look for support.

My concern is that for too many of them we have provided too little of intellectual stimulation and challenge and have aroused too little of the persisting intellectual interest that could ensure their continuing growth as persons, quite aside from success in business or profession. The capacity of such students for personal leadership needs to be supplemented, often, by the kind of intellectual discipline that college should afford. It seems to me likely that many such students might be challenged by the opportunity to move ahead more rapidly, to participate in some of the special honors programs, or to engage in properly directed independent study, or to have a part in projects requiring not only activity but also intellectual application and effort.

Now a final word or two. I have found most interesting and satisfying this participation in the curricular planning in which your faculty is engaged, even though most of my sharing has had to be by letter. I am impressed by the earnestness and the fine spirit which has characterized your procedures. Your committee is not proposing any radical innovations or experimental ventures. Nor am I suggesting any such drastic reforms.

I recall a college dean's telling me once of his reception at one of America's genuinely distinguished liberal arts colleges. He was traveling on a foundation grant which permitted him to visit a number of selected colleges to observe at firsthand what they were doing. When he arrived at _____ College he was told: "You can be sure we are glad to have you. But we really can't understand why you chose to come here. We aren't doing anything new or unusual. We are just trying to be a good college." The visitor soon learned that this did not mean smugness or complacency. I think he came away with more admiration for that college than for any other he saw on his tour.

The experimental college programs which have received publicity—some of them less revolutionary, some of them less enduring than the publicity might have led one to expect—have been interesting and have had stimulus value. But I think the lasting changes that have come about in the American college have not resulted from the adoption of dramatic new plans. I think, too, that the changes that will come and endure in the future will not come suddenly, through some overnight revolution. They will come gradually, through just the kind of work you and your faculty are now doing. What you are engaged in is quite different from what is sometimes called "curriculum tinkering," though this latter process may have its value as you go along. You will not want your curriculum to freeze on you. Occasional modifications and adjustments will probably be needed. This should not be in the least discouraging. It will be a sign of continuing vitality. And it will be all to the good if in five or six years your faculty wants to do another complete overhaul.

Please be sure of my continuing interest and of my warm personal regards and good wishes.

Sincerely,

# 15

## Academic Achievement and Community Resources

Dear President Hosmer:

After the lively discussion in your administrative council during my visit to Caswell last week, I was not at all surprised to receive your letter asking me to comment on the matter of community relations. Your director of development was obviously speaking from the point of view of publicity and fund raising, while the dean's negative attitude reflected his concern over the possible dissipation of faculty time in a host of community activities. The concerns of both officers, in my judgment, are well founded. A faculty can render an outstanding service to the college by participating in selected community activity, but they can also become so involved in such activity that their on-campus responsibilities suffer.

The question you raise, "How can a college utilize community resources to strengthen its academic program?" is evidently a deeper one. It goes beyond the observations of either the development officer or the dean. It has to do with curriculum, teaching method, and the basic nature of liberal learning. I am glad to give you the benefit of my own experience and to tell you of some of my recent observations at several colleges that have been working systematically on this problem.

Without in any sense indicating what Caswell should do, I am convinced that if community resources, human and environmental, can be made to enhance the academic performance of a given institution, they should by all means be turned to account. In utilizing these resources, however, care must be exercised not to substitute pre-professional and vocational courses for activities functionally related to liberal learning. Institutions like Caswell are focused on meeting the long-range needs of maturing intellects; in providing resources for dealing with the unforeseen and the unforeseeable; in broadening horizons and deepening insights; and in disciplining students in hard work and persistent effort. The utilization of community resources must promote rather than jeopardize these academic purposes.

Keeping this philosophy in mind, your dean and faculty might explore ways of utilizing the resources of the Caswell area. When this is done, some very interesting possibilities may appear.

For example, one college I am acquainted with discovered that it could bring new interest in the basic sciences to students and faculty through study, on an interdepartmental basis, of the unusual variety of soils that surrounds the college.

The chemistry department was interested, for instance, in the chemical transformation of parent materials—rocks and vegetable matter—into clays and top soil. The biology department found much to claim its attention in the insects, earthworms and root systems that influenced the structure of the soil, and which also furnished firsthand information on the breeding habits and life cycles of these plants and animals. The physics department found that there were molecular changes in soil particles; that conductivity of heat varied with soils; that the response to electronic stimuli and to light was quite marked; and that the pliable structure of soil could be readily modified. The geology department found that carbon 14 and pollen deposits both dated and helped describe the prehistoric plant and animal content of parent materials being examined.

Needless to say, such team study caused the science division to grow in interest and performance. Papers by faculty and students were read before learned societies, enrollments increased and funds were attracted. The ferment in undergraduate learning spread to other departments and divisions. Faculty members found there was no conflict between teaching and research, and that students could be schooled in independent study and in team methods of gathering data, verifying results and describing their findings.

In like manner this same college, and another in quite a different area, brought new life to the humanities and the social sciences by relating community resources to their academic programs. In the first school, a Bach festival was tied into the music and fine arts offerings, and period studies, courses and performances were utilized to produce a new interest on the campus and a richer appreciation in the community. In the second institution a college-community chorus was organized, a series of art exhibits was set up; and visiting artists, lecturers, educators and others were invited to the campus.

While such activities may draw on local talent and utilize such community resources as are available, there are even more direct ways in which colleges are trying to bring community experience into the classroom.

One institution I visited had organized a cooperative project with a rural high school. This provided internship experience for students in public school teaching, home economics, music, sociology, economics and other fields. During six weeks of residence in the community the interns were supervised by college teachers who visited the high school or assisted in some phase of community activity. In actually working with people, students acquired an understanding of social conditions which they could not possibly have secured from reading and classroom discussions alone. But having had a semester of preparatory study of the economic, sociological and political foundations for an understanding of the problems they were likely to encounter, students were enabled to interpret their experiences more intelligently than would otherwise have been possible. Through this arrangement, faculty members and students did much to raise the educational and economic level of the rural community in which the project was carried on. At the same time they gained fresh insight into their own course materials and were able to share it with other students on their return to the campus.

As you probably know, a modified approach to this sort of field-study internship is being carried on by a number of universities in the Appalachian Mountain Study. Through these contacts, new leadership is being discovered in isolated communities and practical programs of self-help and community development are beginning to appear. But the most interesting result from the academic point of view is what is happening back on the college campuses, where returned students readily challenge textbook and teacher by comparing their field experiences with some of the accepted assumptions. For such students, learning becomes noticeably less concerned with fulfilling course requirements and more with trying to come to grips with actual problems.

By establishing close working relationships with schools, business firms, social agencies and off-campus organizations, and providing careful supervision by competent teachers, it is my belief that such programs can contribute much to a student's education without sacrificing academic rigor.

May I give you another illustration? A midwestern college operated for several years a community improvement program with which I am familiar. The project was closely correlated with classroom instruction in sociology, the sciences and the humanities. Under this arrangement students were brought into firsthand contact with depressed communities and helped to see how they could be made independent and self-respecting. This was done in a county seat, a small town, and mountain communities in Kentucky and Puerto Rico. In these projects the aim was to stimulate intellectual insights and to demonstrate the relevance of liberal arts in community growth.

Reviewing the psychological outcome of this type of instruction, Professor Gordon Allport of Harvard University said: "The joint nature of this inner and outer approach to intellectual and emotional maturity is validated by a series of objective tests and personal interviews." He stated further that the selection factor that this type of education exerts, and the greater motivation that young people feel because of it, provide an experience that changes their lives. He concluded by saying: "This change might have been due to discussion periods, the meditation hour, or the actual physical implementation of ideas; but whatever it was, it worked."

In case you and the dean wish to explore this type of study, I should be glad to furnish testimonials from faculty and students of colleges where such a plan has been in operation for some time. I think you will find they believe that academic validity can be given the program but that this requires a faculty willing to experiment with interdepartmental teaching and the use of field projects. Where this condition is fulfilled, field work should become a regular part of the curriculum, and the director of the program must be a full member of the faculty committee responsible for the activity. In all cases care must be exercised not to emphasize the community development aspects more than the intellectual growth factor. The effort must be kept on an undergraduate level and must help students see the relevance of liberal arts education in a free society.

Still another illustration is the "Master Teacher" plan for prospective teachers. This is designed to instruct liberal arts students in effective classroom methods, while at the same time emphasizing course content. The program makes use of experienced high school teachers who have demonstrated their ability to kindle the enthusiasm of students. They assist heads of departments in the preparation of majors and act as consultants on a two or three hour a week basis. I know of one college that has eight such consultants. Their total cost is about equal to that of one full-time instructor. Where such services are effectively used, the number of students choosing teaching as a profession has increased markedly, and the teacher certification agencies have been impressed with their quality of performance as well as their understanding of the subject matter they are to teach.

Part-time lecturers have also been used by other departments to bring wider experience and enrichment to classrooms. Such lecturers, with Ph.D.'s, broad experience and excellent personalities are generally drawn from business and industry. They work with, or under the direction of, regular staff members, and provide real strength to colleges that otherwise could not afford such help.

And, finally, I am sure you are familiar with the family relations programs that some colleges and communities are developing. These programs relate the liberal arts curriculum, in a collegewide manner, to the problems of family development. A coordinator, giving full time to the program, relates subject matter to the different disciplines and uses family counsellors in the community. He also brings to the institution distinguished anthropologists, psychologists, marriage counsellors and others. He helps make available the problems and experiences of modern family living to various course offerings and, in turn, relates the best in liberal learning to society's most basic institution, the family.

I hope some of the suggestions I have made may be useful to your faculty. It may be that none of them can be applied at Caswell, but whether they can or not, I think you will agree that community resources, if properly utilized, can stimulate academic achievement in the best tradition of liberal education. I hope these observations will reassure the dean and at the same time enable the director of development to see more clearly that community relations have an educational as well as a monetary benefit. I shall be delighted to know whether you give the community resource idea a try at Caswell. It might add a vitalizing dimension to the intellectual life of your students.

Sincerely,

# 16

## Relationships with Students

You are absolutely right in your conviction that a college president must maintain some direct contacts with his students. In no other way can he keep a friendly, understanding relationship with the student body. The big question is just how this can be accomplished without interfering with the responsibilities of other adminstrative officers.

Actually the problem of maintaining sufficient contact to accomplish the essential task is not as difficult as it may seem at first sight. Generally, communication between administration and students leaves much to be desired, no matter how much effort may be put into it. But communication *among* students is extraordinarily effective. The convictions of a small segment of the student body can quickly permeate the consciousness of the great majority of students without any apparent effort at communication.

This phenomenon can be used to presidential advantage. In order that the president may have the confidence and respect of the student body, and may get across to them that he is deeply interested in their welfare, it is not necessary for him to establish direct contact with a majority of the students, much less with each and every student. The desired results may be attained by contacts with seniors only, or with student leaders, or with a random sampling of students.

It is impossible for me at a distance to suggest specifically what you might do to establish better rapport with your students. Even another and lengthier visit to your campus would not give me the prophetic insight that would be needed. There are so many intangibles that must be considered, both as they affect your particular student body and your own qualities of personality and character. It would be rash for me to do more than to pass on to you procedures that have been successfully employed by presidents whom I have met in other colleges. You can then pick and choose, singly or in combination, such procedures as you think might serve in your situation. In short, you must "play it by ear."

I have known presidents, for example, who have made it a practice to teach regularly at least one section of a course, usually with the seniors. It is a very rewarding experience, I can assure you, which will pay dividends not only in student and faculty relationships but also in alumni relations as well. When the president of the college will take time out of his busy schedule to teach a class, the students in the class are not only impressed by the implied importance attached to the particular subject matter but they will take pride in the privilege which they feel has been accorded to them. This seems to be particularly true of seniors, who are about to leave college.

But how can a president teach even one course and attend to fund raising, government relations, meetings, conferences and speeches galore, and internal problems as well? It is not easy, but it can be done and it has been done, even by presidents of some large universities. It requires careful planning. It may involve an arrangement with a faculty member of kindred spirit and of comparable standing in the same subject-matter field. Preferably, the president and this faculty member must arrange to teach different sections of the same class and to communicate and collaborate closely with each other. Schedules will need to be so arranged that the president's classes come at the times least likely to be subject to interference by the urgent demands made upon him. These same hours must needs be left open on the schedule of the collaborating professor, so that he may substitute for the president when unavoidably he must be absent. To balance the arrangement, the president might substitute occasionally in the professor's class. But unless the task, once assumed, can be carried through faithfully, it is better not to undertake it at all. More harm than good will be done if there is apparent inadequate preparation on the part of the president, or if absences are frequent.

Some presidents employ an "open-door" policy with students. Students are given to understand that they are at liberty individually to visit the president whenever any one of them has a problem which he thinks ought to have the president's attention. Any student may gain admission to the president whenever he is in his office and is not in conference. No formality of appointment is necessary. One simply puts in an appearance and informs the secretary in the outer office that one wishes to speak with the president. This policy might seem calculated to make a heavy demand on the president's time. Actually it does not. Comparatively few students will avail themselves of this privilege, either because they realize the president is a busy man and hesitate to take up his time or because they tend to shy away from the "head man." But the fact that students know the door is open to them is in itself beneficial. Of course the president must be careful that students do not use this privilege as a means to bypass other officials.

Where the senior class is not too large, the president may find it possible to schedule a personal interview with each member of the class to inquire about plans for the future, to seek comments about the college in general and to receive suggestions, if any, for improvement. One president makes it a practice to schedule a brief interview with each incoming freshman in the early fall, welcoming him to the college and wishing him well. Where teaching is impossible, such interviews may be of great benefit in establishing more personal relations. This kind of approach to students consumes a lot of time, but presidents who have been able to do it have found it extremely rewarding.

Then there is the problem of what to do about the ever recurring round of student extracurricular events—dinners, socials, entertainments and the like. A president cannot possibly attend them all. Should he make it a practice to accept none of these invitations in order to avoid the implication of showing favoritism for the events he does manage to attend? One president of my acquaintance has answered this question by adopting the policy of rotating acceptances to the various student functions. His policy is well known, understood and accepted by the students. In this way, over a period of two or more years, depending on the number of student functions, a president may find it possible to make at least one personal appearance at each of the various functions. Even with less systematic planning, a president may attend as many college functions as possible without showing favoritism.

Another fruitful means of contact is through student leaders, especially the president of the senior class, the chairman of the student council and the editor of the student paper. Regular appointments are scheduled, when matters of mutual interest can be discussed informally. Thus one president has arranged a weekly conference with the student editor, who may interview him and propose any questions relating to college affairs. The editor is given frank answers to all his questions, with the necessary background information. A full explanation for any administrative action or policy is given when requested, even though it may be necessary to stipulate that it must be considered confidential and off the record for the time being. Any topics discussed which may not be suitable for immediate news release are identified and the reasons for delay are also explained. This president testifies that he has never had reason to regret this man-to-man dealing and that his confidence has never been abused.

Another president, early in the college year, acts as a dinner host to the top student leaders of the senior class. The occasion is a formal one as far as dinner and dress are concerned. Around the table after dinner each student leader talks informally about his particular responsibility, expresses his hopes for the year, identifies the problems which he believes confront him and indicates how he thinks the administration can help. Frankness is the keynote of these talks, even if it seems to involve criticism of the administration. After all the student leaders have had their say, the president comments informally on their remarks. If there is any apparent misunderstanding on administrative matters, the president endeavors to clear it up and to shed light on administrative attitudes and policies.

One president has found that informal evenings which he holds for personnel officials and student government officers at the beginning and end of each semester have been quite effective. At these meetings, administrative-student relationships, including policies on discipline, social activities and community relations, have been discussed and evaluated.

Presidential ingenuity will find many other opportunities for helpful student contacts. Even chance will offer some opportunities if a president is alert to take full advantage of them when they arise. Students may be encountered in corridors or on campus walks. They may even be given a lift by the president when he is driving to or from the campus.

A college president told me that a few years ago he was more or less jockeyed into an informal kind of student contact which had important repercussions. It helped him to solve an immediate personal problem. It also proved to be a source of helpful student relations which carried over into good alumni relations in subsequent years.

He said that after less than a year in the presidency he found the job was getting him down. In order to get back to some semblance of the regular physical exercise to which he had always been accustomed in prior years, he persuaded some of the younger faculty members to take turns joining him for handball or medicine ball and a swim three or four evenings a week. This proved to be the needed tonic for the president and was good while it lasted. But it also proved to be too much of a chore for the young faculty members who served as counselors in residence halls, where they were needed in the evening. But they came up with an alternative suggestion whereby they would recruit some of the older students to provide the necessary competition for exercise. The president had some misgivings about this proposal, but he was assured that the students would be carefully selected. It would be voluntary, of course, and there would be a rotation so that there should be no question of favoritism. He finally agreed.

This proved to be a very successful venture. The president

got his exercise under ideal conditions. The students were more competitive than the faculty members. It was a matter of pride with them that they would not easily permit an older man to beat them in any sport—especially since he was well able to hold his own. Since there was a rotation of students, the president made the acquaintance of some excellent men, good students and leaders, whom otherwise he might never have come to know so intimately.

Never once, the president told me, did any of these students bring up college affairs or make any reference to his position— a welcome change from the faculty members, who could never quite avoid talking shop. As a consequence, the president could completely forget his job and enjoy spirited competition and the light-hearted bantering talk of the students. The president seemed certain that these students had not been coached by faculty members. One student, he said, came to see him in his office about some personal matter which required only a brief interview. The student apologized for the fact that only the evening before he had been with the president at the gym with this matter on his mind and could have asked him then. Nevertheless, feeling that the president probably did not wish to be bothered about official matters at this time, he decided he would take a chance of catching him in his office the following day.

You will note, President Lampson, that all of the contacts I have mentioned are concerned directly with only relatively small groups of students. But when these contacts are properly used, they can do much to spread among the student body a better attitude toward the college administration. Possibly this may take the form of a conviction that the president is a "nice guy" who is really interested in the students. It goes without saying that no president will seek this student acclaim as a personal tribute but only as a means to the effective student cooperation without which a college can make little progress toward the goal of excellence.

Sincerely,

# 17

## Student Personnel Work

DEAR AUBREY:

I am glad to respond to your request for comment on what you refer to as "extracurricular student life."

Probably the reason I have not volunteered any comment on student personnel problems is that I have little confidence in my ability to help with them. This may be partly because I have had less direct experience in this area than I have in others and, frankly, less satisfactory experience with other people's work. My uncertainty may be due also, in part, to the fact that this phase of work with students has come to have a major place in college administration only in comparatively recent years. In earlier years, services to students were less systematized and were in the main an informal responsibility of academic officers and faculty.

Please, then, don't let anything that may sound negative or overcautious in what I say imply denial of the importance of student personnel work. I heartily approve of the attention now given to it in most of our colleges. Yet I cannot refrain from remarking that the increasing recognition being given to these functions has, in my judgment, involved some hazards. Student personnel functions have become professionalized— highly specialized in some of their techniques. The desire for professional recognition has seemed to me to lead to undue emphasis on their claim to administrative status, even at the risk of subordinating the main business of the college. This main business, certainly the unique business, of the college, I still think of as learning and teaching in classroom, library and laboratory.

The officer mainly responsible in this field of student services is usually called "dean of students." In a previous letter I have expressed my conviction that the offices of registrar and director of admissions should be part of the academic administration rather than being placed under the jurisdiction of the student personnel officer. I am well aware, however, that there is disagreement on this point. In any case, even with these two functions eliminated from the area of student personnel services there is still plenty left, and a perplexing and complicated plenty at that.

There is a great deal of student personnel work that cannot be organized for smooth, machine-like operation: the planning, supervision, direction, guidance of all the student's extracurricular (or, if you prefer, co-curricular) life and activities. That many of these activities have educational value can readily be admitted; that such value should be realized as fully as possible is obvious. But am I wrong in saying that responsibility for them, though inescapable, is *incidental* to the main business of the college? It is clear to me, at least, that they should not overshadow or submerge this main business.

Young people are brought together in an academic community. They must be helped in every way possible to mature in personality and in character while on the campus for the primary purpose of achieving the kind of *intellectual maturity* that the college seeks to foster. This intellectual aim distinguishes the college from other social agencies. It is this that justifies its existence: this is what the students are there for. Emotional disturbance, physical illness, defects of personality and character, moral failure can of course interfere with the main business, as can laziness or indifference or misuse of time and energy. Against these we should guard students in every possible way, but always to the end that they may be able to profit by the unique opportunity which is theirs as college students.

Keeping a student body well and happy is important, but it

is not for this that the college exists. Let me quote just one sentence from Harold Stoke: "Perhaps it should be said gently that because it is indispensable, student personnel administration has become something of a cult in its own right with, sometimes, resulting confusion as to whether students are primarily in college to be taken care of or to be educated." (Read his whole chapter on "The President and the Students." You may put an occasional question mark in the margin, as I have done. Nevertheless he says well much that needs saying.)

I must add, even if ungraciously, that there seems to be a tendency for the professionals in this field to become doctrinaire, "impractical theorists," trying to "apply some doctrine or theory without a sufficient regard to practical considerations." (The quoted words are from a dictionary definition of "doctrinaire.") There seems also to have developed a vocabulary—as happens so often with emerging professions or disciplines, a vocabulary that has little or only vague meaning to any one not indoctrinated.

You will, I hope, be able to appoint someone with appropriate professional training, supplemented by an abundance of plain common sense and of tact in dealing with real people, not with abstractions.

Well, the dean of students must have a staff: just how large a staff will "all depend." Sooner or later, probably, there will be need for a dean of men and a dean of women, in addition to the dean of students. Then there must be dormitory house-mothers or supervisors; social counsellors; chaperons; vocational counsellors; fraternity advisers if you are to have chapters of the national organizations or, if not, advisers for the local clubs that will develop. There will be advisers on student publications; medical, including psychiatric, and nursing personnel; experts in a testing and guidance bureau; placement officers to help in getting jobs for students in residence and for prospective graduates. You can doubtless think of others. Obviously some of these staff members will be part-time; some will be unpaid volunteers. Many of these services can be combined under one person. Some of them will be the direct responsibility of one of the other deans, if there is more than one with that title in this area.

For my own satisfaction I must touch on two or three other aspects of this area of service.

There is obvious overlapping in the management and supervision of dormitories, food services and student unions with the work of the business office and its staff. There can easily be trespassing in one direction or the other, and resulting conflict, unless complete understanding and a cooperative pattern of operation have developed.

There is obvious overlapping, also, between the personnel work of the professional staff in this area and the work of the academic dean and the faculty. Here again it is important that there be mutual confidence, the ready sharing of information, and provision for consultation and cooperative planning.

Whose is the responsibility for discipline, i.e., in this instance, the assessment of penalties for misconduct? I have only a few suggestions.

Deans of students often think that they should not have to assume this responsibility, on the ground that it interferes with their more important role as "guide, philosopher, and friend." I am inclined to believe they are right.

Responsibility for punishing offenses in the classroom, such as cheating or plagiarism, should, I think, be the responsibility of the academic dean. He may, very wisely, wish to have the advice of, or even delegate authority to, a faculty committee. If there is an honor system (about which a volume could be written), student members will have authority, either with or without official help and subject or not to official confirmation.

For other offenses against regulations or against standards of conduct set by the college, the dean of students may well wish to depend upon a faculty committee on student conduct, with which he would sit and whose decisions he would execute. Students may or may not be included in such a committee.

All dismissals, expulsions or suspensions should be promptly reported to the president. In my judgment they should be subject to his approval. No wise president will overrule the official decision of a dean or a committee except in extreme cases, and then only after conference with the responsible officers. But he will be the first to receive protests from the family or friends of the student. He cannot escape the final responsibility, and the right of appeal to him as the final authority must be recognized.

It is usually wise to inform parents promptly when students are in serious difficulty, particularly if conflict with the law is involved or there is the probability of suspension or expulsion. Parents, especially parents of younger students, often wish to be advised of academic or personal problems that may jeopardize the continuance of their children in good standing. Certainly all inquiries from parents should be promptly answered.

But not all communications with parents should report difficulties and failures. On the positive side, experience indicates that it means much to parents to receive from the college—a professor, a dean or the president—a note of congratulation on a good record, on some special achievement or recognition, or on some specific evidence of leadership and promise in their children.

And finally, what provision should be made for nurture of the religious life of the students? I shall attempt no extended discussion of this question. I know that it is very close to your heart. So I am sure you will want a college chaplain or a director of religious life. I know that you will choose wisely; that you are sensitive to the need for wisdom, patience and tolerance along with conviction and dedication in such an officer. This officer is sometimes made a member of the staff of the dean of students. There is, however, deep conviction on the part of many leaders that spiritual ministry to students should not be thus subordinated. Circumstances will vary.

In tax-supported colleges this ministry cannot be provided directly by the college. It becomes the extrainstitutional responsibility of the churches, often of course with the approval and cooperation of the college. This arrangement is found also in a good many privately supported colleges and in some church-related colleges or universities of rather complex organization. Under this plan the denominations often name student pastors who cooperate with one another and with officers of the institution. A church-related college, such as yours, cannot abdicate responsibility in this area or delegate it wholly to others— though welcoming on the campus representatives of faiths other than that with which the college is identified.

I feel quite sure that you will wish to have the chaplain or director of religious life related directly to you and responsible only to you. Certainly I do not dissent. I suggest only two things. Even with your vital concern for this ministry, there will be much detail in planning and programming to which you cannot possibly give personal attention. You and this officer will want to keep close to each other, but you must be willing to leave much of the initiative to him. Moreover it is very clear that he must be willing and able to work intimately with the academic dean and the dean of students, with other administrative officers and with the faculty.

It occurs to me now, Aubrey, that you may be smiling as you finish this letter. I have given expression to some pretty definite opinions on a field in which I indicated, to begin with, my lack of confidence in my ability to be helpful. Well, I have smiled a bit myself. As a matter of fact, writing to you has helped to clarify my own thinking and I am grateful for the opportunity.

Until I hear from you again, every good wish, as always.

Sincerely,

# 18

## Public Relations

DEAR PRESIDENT MACLAREN:

It was good to hear from you. I am particularly glad to have you inquire about my attitude toward public relations, since I know that you have heard me express some misgivings about possible overemphasis or misdirection in this field. I suspect that it was *publicity* rather than public relations that I was talking about, and probably in speaking off the cuff, I was not careful enough to make my position clear. The two things, while inter-related, are not identical. Certainly I do not question the importance of good public relations. I do have questions about some of the techniques of publicity that many people regard as making for good public relations.

Let me note first that there are numerous publics to which the college is related in one way or another and in varying degrees of intimacy. Interest, understanding, support on the part of these publics are essential to the continuing effective service of the college. Whether or no we think of campus relationships as "public," I think it is beyond question that communication, understanding, support among the different groups on the campus are fundamental to good public relations off campus. Reports of persistent dissension, factionalism and feuding on campus can affect disastrously the attitudes of the off-campus publics.

I do not need to tell you that all phases of public relations are the inescapable responsibility of the president. The way he handles them will depend upon his individual temperament and special gifts. But it remains true that no one can so effectively and authoritatively interpret the college to the public as can the president. All this you know full well. You have already, during your first few months in office, been devoting a great deal of time and energy to this kind of thing—making many speeches, meeting with varied groups, conferring with officers of foundations, doing much traveling. This has been necessary and you have been most effective. But it is very clear that as you move ahead you will need professional help in this phase of your over-all responsibility.

With this said, I think I can now indicate some of my reservations or apprehensions. I have encountered situations in which it has seemed to me that the area of public relations was having too much influence on policy decisions. Things were being done because it was felt that the public—by which was meant a certain segment of the public—would be pleased. Or, because some people might be displeased, there was hesitancy or failure to discontinue activities that were out of line with professed policy. I am not quite ready to say that public reaction should not be taken into account in advance of a decision. But while such reaction should be anticipated in many instances, this consideration should not be paramount in any case that I can imagine. Policy decisions should be made on the basis of the established purposes of the college and its commitment to sound educational principles. After decision, there should be concern for interpretation to the public of the decision and the reasons for it.

I am suggesting, therefore, that a public relations program, or publicity, is of value when, and only when, it serves to further the educational objectives of the college. There are unobjectionable forms of publicity, I concede, which do not directly or in any large way so serve. Reports to home-town papers on the achievements of students, feature stories about campus activities, visiting speakers, concerts, honors coming to faculty members, to cite just a few examples, keep the name of the college before the public and thus are helpful.

But it is difficult for any reporter to get a good story out of the really important day-by-day work of a college. Thus the things played up are apt to be the unusual, the exciting, even the sensational. Sometimes the sensational is not good publicity; it may be regrettably bad. But any experienced college president can testify that bad publicity is at times inescapable. He will also probably be ready to testify that trying to cover up is exceedingly unwise procedure. He must answer questions with complete frankness, except where the privacy of persons must be protected. Then perhaps all he can do is suffer in silence.

One bit of comfort on this point may perhaps be in order. People forget these things pretty quickly. A new "sensation" always comes along. This fact has of course a less happy implication. People forget the good things too. And a president may sometimes be chagrined to find how little attention has been paid to a really good news story, or how carelessly and uncomprehendingly it has been read.

Most important, and most difficult to achieve, is *understanding*, on the part of those segments of the public that really count, of the educational philosophy, the educational program and the educational achievements of the college. This requires persistent, repetitious, skillful publicity of every available kind.

The first and most important segment of the public whose understanding should be diligently sought is the membership of the board of trustees. An informed and committed board of trustees can be invaluable in interpreting the college to the larger public. As laymen—business or professional men, not academicians—board members can often interpret the college more effectively to those of like background than can the president himself. Where insight and commitment on the part of trustees are lacking, the task of the president is much more difficult.

But for publicity as a whole, the president is ultimately responsible. General policy and much of the detail too must be reviewed by him. But I hardly need to say that, in my judgment, he is most unwise if he thinks of himself, or lets others think of him, as chiefly a public relations officer. His main job is education.

It follows then that you will need effective, even expert, help in the public relations field. I hope you can find a man of such caliber and experience that you can confidently look to him for advice and guidance and entrust to him major responsibility for planning and execution.

I think this officer should be much more than a "publicity man," more than a promoter or propagandist. He must understand and be committed to *educational ideals*. He must be able to interpret them through the written and the spoken word. He should be kept fully informed and should participate in top-level discussions of educational and financial problems. He must be much more than a "rubber stamp" or a "yes-man." He must have ideas of his own, the ability to expound them, and skill in guiding those who work with him. He should, in turn, be expected to keep the president fully informed, to use his insight and skill in guarding the president against blunders and in constructively furthering the educational purposes of the college. At the same time, he and those who work with him must recognize that the final authority is the president's, because his is the final responsibility.

There will be some questions coming up which you have probably anticipated. They have to do with the relationships of your director of public relations to the development office and the alumni office. Activities in these areas are so intimately related that they must be coordinated in some fashion, and those working in them must work *together*. It may well be that until you have gone quite a bit further in finding or training these people, you yourself will have to do the coordinating and take the steps to insure cooperation. I would hope that without undue delay you will be able to have one top-level staff member who can head up, in a single unit, these important inter-related services, again with due recognition of your final responsibility and authority.

I may add that the public relations officer's relationships with other members of your staff and with the faculty will be highly important. Such relationships cannot be formally defined or organized, as can those with the officers more directly concerned with public relations. Little misunderstandings and

trivial irritations are almost sure to occur. But your man will
not be a good public relations man if his own public relations
are not good and if he cannot handle situations in which he
needs to interpret himself and his actions.

I assume that your public relations officer, when you have
found him, will already be well acquainted with the American
College Public Relations Association and the American Alumni
Council. If not, you will certainly want him to make contact
with these national organizations immediately. They are ren-
dering very valuable service, working closely together and
keeping in touch with other organizations with general and
specialized interests in higher education. Their publications
deal not only with techniques but often, most constructively and
imaginatively, with major issues for American higher education.

I hope you can soon find just the right man. If you can,
though it may not be easy, he will be invaluable to you. I am
sorry that just now I cannot suggest anybody who might both
fill the bill and be available, but I will be on the lookout for
possible candidates. In any case, I shall want to hear from you
and I shall look forward to seeing you and talking with you
again.

Every good wish.

Sincerely,

# 19

## Organizing a Development Program

DEAR PRESIDENT MACLAREN:

The fact that your board of trustees, as reported in your recent letter, has authorized you to proceed with all speed in inaugurating a full-fledged development program is a step, but only a step, in the right direction. There is much that must be accomplished before you even think of making a public announcement of your plans.

I can hardly prescribe just how you ought to go about your task, and I am sure this was not your expectation in writing to me. But I can outline for you the measures that most colleges have found it wise to take in setting up a comprehensive development program. It does not follow, of course, that everything I say will necessarily be applicable to your college, because in no two colleges are the situations exactly alike. Nevertheless, the knowledge of what other colleges have done should have at least a suggestive value for you.

In most colleges the completion of an intensive and comprehensive self-study has been the starting point in laying plans for a development program. This self-study differs from that customarily made with a view to accreditation, chiefly because it attempts to project the aims, policies and plans of the college as much as ten or twenty years into the future.

You are fortunate in the self-study which your faculty recently completed as part of the evaluation process for your regional association, a copy of which you were good enough to send me. In it the faculty committee has very ably set forth a clear statement of the present aims of the college. It seems to me that this faculty committee should be reconstituted. Let them project this study into the future, by seeking answers to such questions as: Are these the aims to which the college should hold for the next five, ten or twenty years? Where does the college want to be five, ten or twenty years from now? What is the maximum enrollment for which the college is willing to plan? If there is to be an increase over the present enrollment, what is the target date for reaching the maximum, and what yearly increments are to be planned for in the interval?

Probably you will not wish to wait for the faculty committee to report before getting your trustees and your administrative council to work on these questions. It may be that a committee of the board of trustees could have a few joint meetings with the administrative council and the faculty committee. Suppose that differences of opinion arise among these various groups. This ought not to disturb you. It should not take long to arrive at a consensus, since all minds have been actively at work.

Once agreement has been reached on what ought to be the aims of the college for the next ten or twenty years, and your enrollment goal has been set, you are now ready to make development plans. First you ought to compile a list of your needs for the next twenty years. What additional faculty strength will be needed? What additional facilities in buildings and equipment will be required?

The experience of other colleges suggests that the long-range plan—the planning for what the college should become over a twenty-year period—should be *idealistic*. This means that a college should list the ideal conditions which it would wish to have to do an excellent job of providing education for the number of students projected. At this stage of planning, not too much thought need be given to the over-all cost or how the money is to be raised.

Having completed this long-range estimate of needs, a college then attempts to establish a priority of needs for the next five to ten years. Here *realistic* is the word. This means that the college cannot let idealism override the realism of sound common sense. The critical needs must be accurately judged. The cost must be carefully estimated, but with the proviso that it is better to overestimate a bit than to underestimate. Due allowance must be made for rising costs and the probable need of expanding the preliminary plans for the designated buildings.

It is most important that the main objectives of this five- or ten-year plan be both attainable *and attained*. If the construction target is three buildings, then three buildings must be completed. In setting the financial target for the five- or ten-year effort, the real goal can be missed just as much by setting the sights too low as by setting them too high. Some colleges seem to prefer the risk of setting the target of their financial appeal on the high side. By including in the financial appeal a certain sum of money to increase endowment for building upkeep, they believe they can at least be assured of reaching their building goal.

Colleges with little previous experience in fund raising have found it helpful, if not imperative, to employ professional fund-raising counsel. Especially in the beginning, it is important to have an objective outside appraisal of what money a college can expect to raise, considering all the circumstances of its clientele, its reputation, its standing in the community, and so on. This is where the experience and techniques employed by professional fund raisers are most helpful. When a responsible fund-raising firm has made an objective appraisal of the situation, the verdict they give the college will normally be reliable. It may mean raising or lowering the total sum which the college had in mind, or it may dictate postponing the setting of goals until some necessary preparatory work has been accomplished.

After all their preliminary plans have been completed, many colleges have found that a capital funds drive under professional direction is an effective way to launch a development program. In doing this they have heeded the advice which more experienced colleges have given in warning that one does not complete a capital funds drive and then give attention to launching a long-term development program. The development program ought to begin with the capital funds drive, which is one phase of the over-all program.

A college which has been fortunate enough to identify a faculty or staff member who seems to have the qualifications for heading the development program will have no reason to regret its foresight in assigning such a man to work full time with the fund raisers. Not only will this college be able to insure an uninterrupted and continuous follow-up on the pledges made during the drive, but it will have given "one of its own" background and training that will be invaluable in implementing the continuing development program.

If you succeed in getting your faculty involved in the planning stage of your development program, that will be a good beginning. But watch out that it does not end there! Faculty members are naturally interested in having a say in where the college is to go academically. They are vitally interested in objectives and enrollment goals. But these have no necessary connection in their minds with a development program. They think that anything that has to do with finance is a problem for the president and the administration. So, after your faculty committee has completed projecting its self-study into the future, and this has been discussed by the whole faculty, it is time to take further steps to keep them involved in the development program.

This time it might be well to appoint an *ad hoc* faculty committee to study the various phases of the development program and to suggest how the college might implement the directive of the board of trustees. For practical reasons it would seem advisable that this committee be made up predominantly of younger members of the faculty. It would probably be best to set a date on which the committee's report should be presented to the entire faculty.

If it were my responsibility to appoint such a committee, I should want to see that each member was supplied with a copy of John A. Pollard's *Fund Raising for Higher Education*. This would be my gift to the committee members, with the suggestion that they use it as the basis for committee discussions. There is, of course, a wealth of literature dealing with the various phases of development work, public relations and fund raising. But the Pollard book is, to my mind, the briefest and

clearest exposition, in non-technical language, of the ramifica-
tions of a development program. It also has an undertone of
urgency and an optimism about development programs which
faculty members need to acquire.

Perhaps with a little help and encouragement from you, this
faculty committee may come up with a realistic approach to a
development program. If they sense the importance of coordinating alumni activities, public relations and fund raising,
they will be perceptive enough to suggest a rearrangement of
office space in order to make it possible for these related activities to be brought together in adjoining offices. If they see what
varied possibilities there are for fund raising today, and how
much planning and work are involved, it may be that they can
suggest the pattern of an orderly progress from the comparatively simple to the more difficult and complex. In general, it
makes sense to tackle the tasks that are closer at hand—alumni
giving, parents' funds, and even token student giving.

Let's hope that the committee will see the necessity of making some proposal in the sensitive area of faculty and staff contributions. One college president who, during a long tenure of
office, has conducted several successful drives for funds, told me
that he never went to the public with an appeal for funds until
the people on the campus had made their pledges.

Undoubtedly the faculty committee will see that solicitation
of funds from business firms, industrial corporations and the
like will involve greater preparation and the help of trustees,
advisory boards and prominent friends of the college. They will
recognize also that there are various long-range programs which
will require careful preparation and patient cultivation on the
part of many individuals—programs, for example, that deal with
special gifts, wills, bequests and certain types of estate-planning
that can be designed to help a college.

It may be that your *ad hoc* committee will suggest permanent
faculty committees to cooperate in various phases of the development program. But I would not be too concerned with this
until your plans are more clearly developed. The important task
of the committee at this stage is to convince faculty members

both of the importance of the development program and of the necessary part which the faculty must play.

I have said nothing about the cost of this program. It is too early to talk about a budget in anything but the most general terms. Whatever can be said about a budget at this time must be derived from the experience of other colleges. You must be prepared for the fact it costs money to raise money, even voluntary gift money. Those with experience estimate the cost of special gift campaigns to be at least ten to fifteen cents for each dollar raised. For continuous development programs, colleges generally estimate the cost to be six to eight per cent of the college budget. It is, of course, safe to predict that the cost ratio will be much higher until a program is well established.

Although I began this letter with the statement that I could "hardly prescribe just how you ought to go about your task," it would seem that a rather lengthy "prescription" has been written. But in talking directly to your situation—even "prescribing" what I think ought to be done—I console myself with the thought that the advice has actually been gleaned from the experience of many colleges. May I look forward to a report from you?

Sincerely,

# 20

## A Director of Development

DEAR PRESIDENT MACLAREN:

As you ask, I am quite willing to outline the qualifications you ought to look for in a director of development. Also I will do everything possible to find you a suitable candidate for the job. I must be very frank in saying, however, that even though you could find the ideal man (a not very likely assumption, I assure you), you cannot possibly divorce yourself from development work and fund raising.

This has been the president's job from the beginning. Certainly now, the big donors and the important people who can allocate funds to colleges want to see the president. A development director will, of course, handle many of the details and do all the preparatory work, but when the chips are down and there is big money at stake, the president becomes a very important member of the development staff and must take his assignments. I know of no college that has an effective program where this is not the case.

It will, in fact, be easier for you to divorce yourself from other facets of college administration than from the development program. I believe this was at least intimated to you in previous correspondence. But you want my ideas on the qualifications of a director of development, not a lecture on presidential responsibilities.

I must confess that it is easier to talk about presidential responsibilities than it is to list the qualifications for a director of development. I recall once seeing such a list, but I doubt it would be much help to you, because it seemed to demand a veritable superman. Actually the qualifications have to be based on what the job requires at your particular institution. Of course there are certain general qualifications which would be needed in heading up a development program at any college. But let us begin with the requirements of the job at your college.

First, there is your alumni situation. It is generally conceded that the alumni program belongs within the ambit of development and public relations. The alumni program is the oldest and most independent segment of this area of administration, if not also the most important. Yet there can be only one head to this area of administration, under the president. This is your director of development. So he must be a diplomat, with sufficient intelligence, prudence, tact, personality and persuasive ability to bring the alumni organization completely into his administrative area, in order that all alumni efforts will be coordinated with the over-all development program. Furthermore, this must be accomplished without creating the impression of taking over the alumni organization, dictating alumni policies, interfering with alumni independence or diminishing the prestige of the alumni secretary. All this implies the ability to organize and direct others with understanding, patience and perseverance.

Then there is your public relations office. This also must come under your director of development without demoting the present man or seeming to degrade his position. But the whole idea of public relations will have to be enlarged, and it must be completely coordinated with all fund raising and planning, whether short-term or long-term. I am unable to say whether or not additional qualifications are indicated here. But certainly none of the qualifications already mentioned can be dispensed with.

Somehow or other, your director of development must convince the alumni secretary that the new administrative setup will mean a big step forward for the alumni association and give new importance to his own position and prestige. (The alumni executive board will have to be dealt with in appropriate fashion, but I will not pursue this here, because I assume it will be the president's task.) In similar fashion, the public relations officer must be inspired with the idea that under the new setup public relations will now come into its own and become more important and more appreciated than ever before.

In brief, both alumni secretary and public relations officer must feel that they, with the new director of development, are now members of a team working for the greater progress and fame of the college. They must concede leadership to the director of development because of his dynamic qualities and the fact that he is chock-full of worthwhile ideas.

The director of development must, of course, have the fullest support from all the members of your immediate college family, from the board of trustees, from the officers of administration and all their assistants, from all members of the faculty and from the students. To obtain this support he will have to work with all of them intimately. Again, he must have a thorough knowledge of and commitment to the ideals and objectives of higher education and he must be, or at least become, dedicated and enthusiastic in his attachment to the college. Of course, he must be an imaginative thinker and a practical psychologist.

It is difficult to list further qualifications, but it must be apparent to you, as it is to me, that the man you are seeking to head up your development program need not really be a superman—just an all-round man who could succeed in almost any administrative undertaking. He ought to be the kind of man who has the abilities to serve as an academic dean, a competent business manager or a top-notch dean of students.

Do you wonder that it is so difficult to find an experienced man with all these qualifications? It is especially difficult when so many colleges are seeking men for the same administrative post. But I suppose you will not be satisfied if I do not make some suggestions as to how you might go about finding somebody suitable.

You could write to the executive director of the American College Public Relations Association. He might know of a promising young man holding a junior post in the development office of a large institution who is looking for an opportunity to be on his own at a smaller college. Occasionally there may be an experienced development director at a large institution who, for one reason or another, wishes to move to a smaller institution. I know of one small liberal arts college that was fortunate enough to find such an experienced director. After years of bedevilment with the pressures and cross-fires of a large institution, this man had decided henceforward to devote his life and energies (at a reduced salary, of course) to a small college.

I know of another small college which, on the insistence of a member of the board of trustees, made an enticing offer to a man employed in development work at a larger institution. The only visible result was that the institution where he was already employed improved his title and raised his salary to such a point that he could not afford to leave. Even if you could pay a handsome salary to a man with the qualifications you want, but now in the employ of another college, I do not think you would want to do it that way. After all, you have to live with your conscience.

Occasionally a college has found a good development director on the staff of a professional fund-raising organization. But there is a risk in that. Unless you know your man well, and unless he has already proved himself at your college (during a capital funds drive, possibly as the representative of his company), you might get a man who was not sufficiently motivated. He might be looking chiefly for a place to settle down with his wife and children after the rough life of being shifted from city to city on fund-raising assignments. He might lack the specific ability and that personal interest in and enthusiasm for the college which are so necessary in a director of development. Undoubtedly his experience would be a valuable asset, but no amount of experience would compensate for a lack of dedicated motivation. Also, the man who heads up the fund-raising activity of a college should be at least as much interested in educating youth as he is in raising funds and promoting the college.

To my way of thinking, all this suggests that your best chance to find a development director lies *within your own staff*.

Forget about experience! Find a man who has the right qualities and let him get his training and experience on the job. If he is a young man, don't give him the title "Director of Development," much less "Vice President." You may either scare him to death or build up his ego too quickly. In either case you will make it very difficult for him to deal successfully with other administrators and the faculty. If you can find the right man, appoint him as your assistant and then let him learn the job with the considerable help of the American College Public Relations Association and the American Alumni Council. Meanwhile, I am afraid, you yourself will have to take over for a time the complete responsibility of director of development.

I'm sorry, President Maclaren; I know this is not the answer you want. But I must be honest with you—and I see no other way out of it.

Sincerely,

# 21

## The President and the Development Program

DEAR PRESIDENT MACLAREN:

My reply to your recent letter has been delayed a bit because I wished to find out whether or not the Howard Eckly I had in mind as a suitable prospect for your development program was still available. I regret to report that he is already signed up with Murchiston College.

Good men with experience and ability in college development work have always been difficult to obtain, but now it is practically impossible to find them at any price. Eckly was available only because he inherited an impossible situation at Lackland. Both the alumni office and the public relations office considered themselves quite independent of the new development office, and the president was either unable or unwilling to clear up the situation. Up to the last minute Eckly, who was a Lackland graduate, hoped that the president and the board of trustees would resolve the difficulty, and so he made no attempt to line up another position.

Do you think you are ready to engage a "go-getter" like Eckly, even if you could find the right man? I confess that I have some reservations on that point. Your alumni office functions independently of the college. It draws its support directly from alumni sources. The alumni secretary will be more responsive to the executive board of the alumni association than to the college or to you. Of course your public relations man is directly responsible to you. If he were a suitable prospect to head up a new development office, your problem would be eased somewhat. But we both seem agreed that in personality he is not suitable. There is also the long-standing friction between the alumni secretary and the public relations director to be considered.

Even if your public relations man had the ability, which both of us question, he could hardly serve as director of development in the circumstances. But both the public relations director and the alumni secretary have served the college, each in his own way, for many years. It would not be possible to bring in a new director of development, no matter how competent, and expect him to coordinate the activities of these two offices. It would just be a case of the Lackland situation over again.

Does that mean that you are stymied in your plan to organize a development program, now that you have a green light from the board of trustees? I don't think so. You can move ahead with your program. It simply means that you will have to assume personal charge and personal responsibility for this program, at least until it is well established. Even under ideal conditions and with a top-flight development director at your command, you would still have to play a considerable part in the development program, as indeed I have been insisting from the outset.

Although it may be a little rough on you for a while, it really is not a bad thing that you should have to dig into this development work at firsthand. The program will be all the stronger and the college will greatly benefit. As a matter of fact, no one but you can bring this alumni situation in hand. You have worked successfully with both the alumni secretary and the public relations director. They will have no reason to resent your inaugurating a full-scale development program. In fact I think they will breathe a sigh of relief. Don't overlook the fact that the action of your board of trustees in approving a development program brought a flock of rumors to the campus.

Be patient with me! I understand your amazement that, knowing as I do how overworked you are, I suggest you take over personally the inauguration of a development program. Of course, considerable adjustments will have to be made in your present duties. You will have to divest yourself of many of the details which you now handle personally. You will have to delegate more responsibility to other staff members. You will have to reduce considerably your numerous speaking engagements.

For example, the dean and the department heads could be given more responsibility in recruiting new faculty members. The business manager could certainly handle many of the financial details which now have your personal attention. Why not bring some of your outstanding faculty members to public attention by diverting to them the flood of speaking invitations that come to your desk? You can hand-pick the speakers for the various assignments. It will be excellent public relations for the college.

Finally, get yourself a personal assistant. You will not have to look far afield for one. That young assistant professor of English whom you recently engaged appeals to me as an excellent prospect. You may have a job to persuade him to leave teaching —he is in love with it—but you are a competent persuader. He impresses me as the type of young man who would make a good assistant. He is alert and bright and has an excellent personality. You may find eventually that he will be the answer to your prayer for a good development director.

If you should decide to appoint him, I would leave the "development" angle entirely out of the picture for the present. You can appeal to him on the basis of the excellent administrative experience he would have as your assistant. You can give him single assignments to do in the beginning, entirely apart from the development work, to try out his tact and initiative. Then you could send him to represent you at meetings of the American College Public Relations Association and of the American Alumni Council, with instructions to report back to you in detail as to what went on at these meetings. By his grasp of the problems discussed and his incipient enthusiasm, you can judge his possibilities for development work.

Assuming that you will make progress in removing some of

the roadblocks to a comprehensive development program, including the alumni situation and faculty lack of interest, you can inject your assistant more and more into the program as your representative. But until you are sure of your man and confident that the local situation is right, it will be necessary for you to be personally involved in the program, working side by side with him and retaining primary responsibility. Within two years, I am willing to wager, your assistant will be able to take over. Meanwhile you will have been thoroughly educated on all the ins and outs of a development program and will be able to give him the encouragement and backing that he will need.

Finally, a few words on the alumni situation—your biggest and most crucial problem. It will take all your ingenuity and powers of persuasion to resolve it. But I think you can show the alumni how much their association will benefit, as well as the college. By seemingly giving up a little independence, the alumni association will actually gain far more in prestige and support from the college.

Show them your plans for the new office arrangements in the administration building. Explain why the first floor of one wing is to be given over completely to alumni, public relations and fund-raising offices. Point out that there will be a joint service office with duplicating machines, addressograph equipment and files, an adequate storage room and a commodious conference room.

What an improvement this should be for the alumni office after it has been isolated these past few years in those cramped basement quarters of the classroom building! With all these important administrative offices on the one floor it will be possible to bring about much needed improvement in communications. It will be possible also to centralize addressograph files and avoid expensive duplication. The registrar can hardly object to turning over to the alumni office the addressograph plates of the class just graduated, since these will be available in the same building and on the same floor.

If there are still objections to the college taking over the alumni office as an integral part of the administration and with

alumni personnel on the college payroll, don't give up. I know
of one college where the alumni association was separately incorporated and legally independent of the college. Understand-
ably, there were objections to abandoning this setup. But a
compromise arrangement was worked out. A formal agreement
was entered into between the alumni corporation and the college corporation whereby the alumni body agreed to suspend
its autonomy on a trial basis for a period of five years, in order
to operate as a closely related unit of the over-all development
program. The alumni secretary, with whom I talked a few
months after this arrangement went into force, was quite enthusiastic about the change and confided to me his conviction
that they would never go back to the old system. After the five-
year trial period was up, he was sure, the separate alumni corporation would simply be permitted to lapse.

In talking with alumni, don't hesitate to drop the idea
discreetly that the present alumni setup is completely out of
step with modern alumni thinking and practice. You can cite
many examples to drive home this point. It may be that you
can get one of the chief executives of the American Alumni
Council to talk to an alumni meeting or at least to the executive
board. He will support your stand with facts and figures. He
ought to carry a lot of weight with your alumni because of his
position and experience. At least he cannot be accused of having a personal axe to grind.

Before closing, and lest you have any doubts about the feasi-
bility of training your own development director, let me say
that the most successful development directors have come up
from faculty or administrative personnel of colleges. If you can
select from your own organization one who has the personality,
the initiative, the enthusiasm and the willingness to learn, the
opportunities for training on the job are excellent.

Both ACPRA and the American Alumni Council are doing
superb work in stimulating and educating development directors. This is accomplished chiefly through regional and national
meetings, through workshops, and through a stream of publications dealing with "what to do" and "how to do it," compiled
from the experience of successful college programs. I have been

impressed with the remarkable *esprit de corps* of those who are engaged in either public relations or alumni work. They are most willing, even anxious, to pool experiences and to help one another. A young man just starting out will get invaluable help from these organizations. Furthermore, he will find an open door and a helping hand from the devolopment personnel in almost any college he may choose to visit.

There is so much still unsaid that it is difficult to bring this letter to a close, but I do not wish it to be too long. So please feel free to ask any other questions that may come to mind. I shall be very happy to write to you again.

Sincerely,

# 22

## Development Program and
## the Faculty

Dear President Soames:

It is a matter of real regret to me that I cannot attend your faculty convocation, to speak on the inauguration of your development program. My schedule is already booked tightly for the next two months. Since you probably can't wait until I could meet with you, perhaps you could arrange for somebody from the Council for Financial Aid to Education to be your guest speaker. Failing this, why not set the ball rolling yourself? You can do it as well as any outsider.

For what it may be worth, I will tell you how I have approached this problem with other faculty groups. In some instances I have found that the faculty response has been very good. In other instances I have not been quite sure what the reaction was, although the presidents concerned have assured me later that the net result was helpful. On such occasions my approach is indirect. I never permit myself to be billed for a talk on the development program. I agree to talk informally to the faculty on "Current Concern for Higher Education" and ask that part of the time be devoted to a question or discussion period. A brief outline of the talk would run something like this.

Today higher education is the object of greater concern on the part of the general public than ever before. Essentially the reason for this concern is the unprecedented rise in the number of high school graduates seeking admission to college. This has created a shortage of facilities in the colleges that will require extraordinary efforts to meet in the foreseeable future. At the same time, there is a general conviction on the part of all citizens that a college education is more necessary than ever before. It is necessary if we are to keep up with the unparalleled scientific advances in a highly mechanized society. It is necessary if we are to retain our leadership and even hold our own in a world of international competition. Furthermore, it is necessary if we are to meet the critical need of ensuring our very survival in a nuclear age.

Fortunately, there is a very favorable climate of opinion at the present time for voluntary giving to colleges and universities, whether privately or publicly supported. This fortunate situation is, of course, no accident. It is largely the result, I am convinced, of the efforts of various public-spirited agencies which have used all communication media to dramatize the situation. They have alerted the general public to the needs of higher education and have convinced the various segments of the public of their respective obligations to support higher education. I believe a great share of the credit for the present favorable attitude toward voluntary giving is due to the Council for Financial Aid to Education, the American Alumni Council, the American College Public Relations Association, the Independent College Funds of America, the United Negro College Fund, and the various agencies that have cooperated with them, such as the Advertising Council of America, the N. W. Ayer Company, and others.

Having thus set the stage, I digress at some length to tell about the Council for Financial Aid to Education. This council is described as the most encouraging phenomenon that it has been my good fortune to encounter in a long educational career. Then I tell about the origin of the council: how it was started, not by educators, but by top-flight industrial and business leaders who were concerned about the future of privately supported colleges and wanted to do something to help. Some of these leaders are named in telling how they came together, how they incorporated and constituted themselves a board of directors.

Later this board was enlarged to include educators, who now make up one third of the directors. Reference is made to their small but able and dedicated headquarters staff, and sidelights are given on the background of the chief officers. From there it is an easy step to talk about the threefold task this council has undertaken.

The council endeavors to convince business and industry of the stake they have in the future of higher education and of the necessity of giving generous financial aid. It assists business and industry with research and studies on legal and tax matters as these have a bearing on corporation gifts to higher education.

The council also endeavors, with the assistance of the public relations media, to alert the general public, not only to the situation of the colleges, now and for the foreseeable future, but to the necessity for generous voluntary support.

Finally the council seeks to convince colleges of the necessity of organizing for voluntary support and encourages them to take appropriate action by informing them of the most practical and successful techniques. The contacts with colleges have been made chiefly through a series of highly organized seminars for college presidents, and sometimes for college trustees, held in convenient locations throughout the country. An enthusiastic description of the conduct of one of these seminars is then given, with possible mention of the fact that the local college president has attended one of these seminars and would undoubtedly be able to confirm my own judgment.

Since there is no doubt that the council, with the aid of the various communication agencies, has done a superb job, I give a rapid rundown of some of the instances in which members of the faculty may have come in contact, by radio, television, billboard or poster, with evidences of the council's activity. It is possible to mention some of the influential communication media which have donated time and space as a public service. In this way, the modest budget of the council for public relations purposes has produced many millions of dollars' worth of the very highest type of public relations activity.

I have no fear that this rather lengthy digression will bore faculty members, because usually it is completely new and interesting information for them. It is then easy to get back to the main line of thought by demonstrating that the dedicated activities of CFAE and other agencies for the past several years are now paying off.

Federal and state agencies are making available yearly to colleges and universities many millions of dollars through loans, grants and various contractual relations. Added to this, there are millions of dollars in direct government aid to students, through loans, grants and scholarships. Voluntary giving from private sources has also increased by leaps and bounds. Annual alumni contributions to colleges have already passed the two hundred million mark and the end is not in sight. Corporations in business and industry are rapidly approaching the two hundred million in annual contributions to colleges. Add to this foundation gifts, individual donors among the wealthy and not so wealthy, parents who contribute over and above the substantial amounts charged for the education of their children, and you have some idea of the concern of the public for higher education. For 1960-1961, it was estimated that voluntary support of America's colleges and universities amounted to over one billion dollars. By 1970 it is hoped that voluntary contributions from all sources will have reached an annual total of more than two billion dollars.

It is easy to make the point that this largess does not come to colleges as a matter of course. They must work for it, and work for it in a way that is purposeful, systematic and well coordinated. All the evidence indicates that any college, no matter how small, no matter where situated, and no matter under what auspices it may be conducted, can successfully obtain needed support if it is doing a good educational job and if it will get organized properly and go to work. But only institutions that are alert, that are willing to pay the price of efficient organization, will succeed in obtaining a proper share of the support that is available.

I then go on to point out that because of this favorable climate for voluntary giving and because of the considerable preparatory work that has already been done, entirely apart from the individual college, it would be rash and foolhardy for any college to pass up the opportunity to raise faculty salaries and to build the necessary physical facilities. Furthermore, time is running out. Institutions that lag behind in their development efforts are missing the boat; they will soon find themselves outdistanced by other colleges which have developed more appealing programs and have been able to attract financial support and to compete successfully for high-quality students. Continuous programs of development and fund raising have long since passed the experimental stages. There is plenty of information available on methods and techniques for any college that wants it.

This kind of organized activity is usually carried on under the name "Development Program." This term has now come to designate a whole new area of college administration, which embraces at least three basic activities: alumni and alumnae affairs; public relations and publicity; and fund raising of every type. Although these activities are not new in themselves, their coordination and the new techniques used are comparatively recent.

It is important to make clear to the faculty that the success of a development program is not simply the responsibility of the president of the college and the administrative officers. Unless it involves *everyone* connected with the college, unless it has the interest and support of the board of trustees and any auxiliary council, all the administrative officers, the faculty, the non-academic staff, the students, the alumni and friends of the college, a development program will hardly get off the ground.

I try to watch the time carefully so as to leave at least one third of the whole session for discussion. It is this discussion period that enables the speaker to show how the faculty can, and must, support a development program. Almost invariably, the discussion turns out to be lively, with searching questions about faculty responsibilities. Often opposition will be vigorously expressed. Faculty people typically believe that their job is to teach, to do research and to publish, whereas finding money to operate the college and to provide the needed facilities is, they think, the responsibility of the administration. Not unnaturally, perhaps, this attitude has tended to stiffen as the administrative apparatus of colleges has grown. But I believe it can be cogently answered.

If a faculty member cannot see that contributing to the development program is part of his responsibility as an educator, he may be persuaded to recognize that helping higher education is part of his duty as a citizen. If he argues that development is not *his* job, that he is not paid to do that kind of work, he may be asked to reflect that the industrialists who secure the support of their confreres for higher education, the trustees who work for the good of the college, the alumni who labor for the alumni fund are not paid, either, for these services to the college. In doing what they do, they are helping the college to increase its resources for the support of programs that are very much the business of the faculty.

Faculty members sometimes get the mistaken impression that participation in a development program necessarily involves their personal solicitation of money. Not only would this be distasteful to them in most instances, but they may well be unfitted by temperament and experience for this particular task. On the other hand, many executives of foundations whose support is sought for educational and scientific projects wish to hear those projects explained by the faculty members who are to conduct them. Often these foundation people would rather rely for information on professors who are authorities in the relevant fields of study than on the director of development or even on the president. Other prospective donors may be no less influenced by faculty interest and enthusiasm.

The key role of the faculty, however, is in the *planning* that should underlie a development program. No such program is worth much unless it rests on a clear formulation of the aims of the college for the foreseeable future and the academic programs through which those aims are to be attained. That is why many colleges undertake a thorough-going self-study before embarking on a development program. Academic planning should precede consideration of ways and means, but in establishing a development program the two processes are closely interrelated and continuous. For that reason, the faculty should ideally be involved at every stage in the development program.

I am afraid I have gone beyond the brief outline I promised you earlier in this letter. But I appreciate your problem and I want to help. It is easy to understand your impatience with faculty indifference, because you know that the prime beneficiaries of a development program will be the faculty themselves. If, as often happens, however, they don't realize this fact, the problem is fundamentally one of communication. You are now reaping the results of poor communication between administration and faculty in the past. Once your faculty members see how much their voice must be heard in planning for the future and in interpreting the needs of the college to others, once they understand how much they have at stake in this endeavor, you will find a considerable change for the better.

When my schedule does permit me to visit your campus, I shall be very much interested to see what progress the development program has made. Meanwhile, if there are any matters we can discuss by letter, do not hesitate to write.

Sincerely,

# 23

## *Business Management*

DEAR AUBREY:

It was good to learn that you found my suggestions about your administrative organization helpful in your planning. It is true that I did not go into much detail about business management as an important phase of the operation of a college. I am glad to comply with your request that I write further on this aspect of your administrative problems.

You are fortunate, as I have already suggested, in being in a position to choose your own chief staff members. Many a president has been harassed and handicapped by coming into a situation in which relationships and procedures were already set, or by inheriting associates committed to familiar ways of doing things and unwilling or unable to change.

You are fortunate also in that there are now available, as was not true in my early days as a college president, exceedingly valuable and helpful guides in this whole area of fiscal and business management. If you bring in a man who has already had experience in college and university business administration, he will most certainly be familiar with these publications. He will also have had intimate contact with the national and regional organizations of business officers and with the consulting service conducted by them. If, on the other hand, you find it desirable to bring in someone experienced in business but not in college business, you will want him very promptly to familiarize himself with these publications and make contact with these organizations: *College and University Business Administration* (two volumes, 1952 and 1955), published by the American Council on Education; the National Federation of College and University Business Officers Association, uniting five regional organizations; the National Federation Consulting Service. *College and University Business* is a periodical which the business manager and, for that matter, the president will find both useful and interesting.

I might very well stop with this bit of steering toward reliable sources of help. Nothing has come out to supersede the authoritative manual which details accounting and reporting procedures that are now widely, if not universally, followed. The associations, the national federation and the consulting service, with the publications available under their auspices, will prove indispensable aids to your business manager.

But, as you go forward with your plans, it may be helpful to you to have a few hints from me as to some things to be on the lookout for: one or two direction signs, maybe, with occasional warnings. Noting them here will indicate the importance I attach to them as a result of my own experience and my fairly intimate acquaintance with situations in a number of other colleges.

First, then, the officer to whom you can with confidence delegate major responsibility for fiscal and business operations of all kinds must be a good businessman. But there are certain reservations here. He must recognize that all the business operations of the college are carried on in the interests of the educational program of the college. He must accept the fact that economy and efficiency, highly desirable as they are, cannot always be measured in the running of a college by the same standards that would serve in the operation of a business for profit. Briefly, your business manager must be interested in education as well as in business. He must be concerned to see to it that business operations serve an educational end.

My second concern is that your business manager keep you, as president, informed through regular reports at stated intervals and in response to such special inquiries as you may have occasion to direct to him. This is for me a fundamental principle: the business manager's actions must always be subject to the approval of the president and, of course, of the board of trustees, to whom the president is in turn responsible. I once knew of a business manager who remarked in an off-guard moment: "It's part of our job to keep the president from finding out how much money we actually have." No president should tolerate any covering up of facts or withholding of information. Nor should a president tolerate for long any disposition to dictate fiscal policy to him, though he should welcome advice and guidance in those areas in which his own competence is apt to be limited.

The chief business officer should *share* in the process of budget-making. I do not believe, however, that he should be thought of, or should think of himself, as the chief budget officer. He should not be in a position to override the president or the dean in matters of policy—and the budget is in a very real sense an important policy document. Final authority and responsibility in budget-projection are the president's, subject again, of course, to approval by the governing board or its authorized committee.

The business manager can be exceedingly helpful in providing information and in supervising the mechanical details of processing the budget. He should have his say in budget conferences. It is the responsibility of the business manager, of course, to control expenditures in accordance with the approved budget. This may at times subject him to pressures and even to harsh criticism from faculty members. Against unfair attitudes the president should protect the business manager by making clear to the faculty, and perhaps to others, including students, the procedures involved in budget-making and the responsibility of the business manager for holding the line laid down in the budget. But in more than one instance I have encountered comments by external survey teams to the effect that the business manager was having *too much* to say about the budget.

In the handling of investments, the president should arrange for the business manager to work closely with a committee of the governing board—a committee on investments, or on finance, or on endowment. It is hardly necessary for me to add that here too the president should be kept fully informed and should share responsibility for major decisions.

Beyond the two major functions just touched on, handling investments and dealing with budgetary matters, there are other areas of business management in which high competence is required: accounting, purchasing, plant operation and maintenance, auxiliary enterprises, among others. This implies that your business manager will need qualified assistants in some of these specialized areas. Some of these distinguishable business functions can, of course, be combined under a single officer. Some of them, according to his preference or his special interest, may be handled directly by the chief business officer. One encounters a variety of such combinations. I am not prepared to say just how much of a staff your business operations will require to begin with.

As the college grows and business operations become more complex, expansion of the business office staff will undoubtedly be necessary. In this expansion, you will run the risk of being charged with developing a top-heavy administration. But given proper attitudes on the part of the business staff, faculty members can be brought to see the necessity of efficient handling of the variety of business details *in the interest of educational efficiency.*

It is obvious that the chief business officer must be able to work understandingly and cooperatively not only with the president but also with the other major administrative officers, with his own staff and with the teaching faculty. There are numerous overlappings of his responsibilities with those of others. These can sometimes make for misunderstandings and even for serious conflict. Handling these, when they develop, will demand of the president a combination of firmness and tact.

Perhaps the comment I now make will have no relevance to your situation, since you are in a position to have a hand in drafting bylaws for the new college and thereby to determine its administrative pattern. I call your attention, however, to the fact that in a good many institutions—fewer now, I think, than in the past—there is a treasurer, appointed by the governing board and directly responsible not to the president but to the board itself. I could cite several instances in which this dual headship has been productive of serious conflict. I have no reservation in saying that, in my judgment, *all* administrative officers should be nominees of the president and directly responsible to him. In an occasional college the president himself is also the treasurer. This is better than the dual lines of direct relationship to the board, but it is apt to impose detailed responsibilities on the president which he had better not have.

Let me add that my insistence on what I conceive to be the proper relationship between the president and the business manager does not imply that the business manager should be completely blocked off from direct contact with the board or its committees. My point is that this officer should not be in a position to go around or over or behind the back of the president. Such direct contacts as he has with the board should be arranged or approved by the president.

My chief concern is that you should have *one man*—your own choice—to whom other business officers are directly responsible, upon whom you can rely for advice and to whom you can entrust responsibility for direction and supervision of multifarious business operations, ranging from the investment of perhaps millions of dollars and the receipt and disbursement of income from a variety of sources to the provision for parking space, the repair of leaky roofs, building a new bookcase for a professor's office or improvement of the menus in the dining hall.

Now, Aubrey, as I read over this letter, it looks as if I have overdone the warnings and put too much emphasis on possible difficulties. The difficulties are not imaginary: they have actually been encountered. My main concern, however, is to urge the importance of the business manager in your administration. I want you to find the man you need, have clear understandings with him and then *lean on him*. He can be of tremendous help to you. I have known many business officers who were not only efficient but also as dedicated to the educational ideals of their colleges as any president or dean or faculty member could possibly be. This kind of dedication sometimes runs through the whole organization and finds expression in the attitudes of janitors and dishwashers as well as on higher levels of responsibility. To such people, in every echelon of service, college presidents owe and readily avow a debt of gratitude.

I am wondering, as I close this letter, if there are any other aspects of administrative organization on which you might wish my comment. If so, please call on me. I want to keep in touch.

Sincerely,

# 24

## Publishing Financial Statements

Dear President Fenwick:

In your recent letter you raise a question as to the publication of financial reports which has arisen out of a disagreement with your director of development. I do not like to take sides against you, but in this instance I cannot agree with your position. I think your director of development has the right point of view. It seems to me important for the college to publish an annual financial report for general distribution.

Experience has proved that money is available to help the college that will make the necessary effort to win such support. Part of the basis of appeal is willingness to put the financial cards on the table. This is necessary in appealing for annual alumni giving and for parents' funds, in seeking gifts and grants from friends and benefactors, from business, industry and foundations.

There is no reason why you should hesitate to make your financial difficulties public. This will be no reflection on your administration. It is commonly accepted today that no college worthy of the name can operate on what is received from students in tuition charges and fees, and few, if any, colleges can depend on their endowments to make up the difference. No practicable raises can be expected to keep pace with the rising cost of education. There is a limit beyond which tuition charges cannot be raised without putting a college education beyond the reach of the majority of students.

Fortunately, business, industry, government and the general public are well acquainted with the situation because of the vigorous educational campaigns of various public-spirited organizations. That is why industrial and business concerns and philanthropic foundations, when awarding scholarships to students, often make supplementary grants to the colleges which these students elect to attend, in order to bridge the gap between tuition charges and the cost of education.

But before you publish a financial statement for general distribution, make sure that your business office and your auditors are using the fiscal and accounting practices commonly followed in college and university accounting. Otherwise your published financial statement will not be a "comparable statement"— that is, not like the financial statements issued by other colleges. Unless it is comparable it may give misleading and erroneous impressions and thus do more harm than good.

So make certain that the public accounting firm engaged by the college to audit the books is familiar with college accounting procedures. Furthermore, insist that the financial report which they prepare observes the standard forms and terminology recommended by *College and University Business Administration,* a publication of the American Council on Education. In college accounting, as contrasted with commercial accounting, there are rather important differences. Thus the terms "profit" and "loss" are not used; "surplus" has a different connotation; depreciation of buildings, furnishings and equipment is not taken unless actually funded, and so forth.

You cannot rely merely on the knowledge that your accounting firm serves other colleges. I know of three colleges served by the same auditors which had reports of three different types. Only one report followed the customary college forms and procedures and was, in my opinion, satisfactory.

In publishing a financial statement, no college presents the entire auditor's report. I feel certain that your director of development did not mean the entire report. If by any chance he did mean this, I should have to take strong exception. Publishing the entire report would be expensive and would serve no useful purpose. In fact it would defeat the whole purpose of publishing a financial statement, because few people would take the trouble to read it, and of those who did read it still fewer would really understand it.

The statement to be published ought to be brief and presented as simply as possible. Unless it can be read and understood it will serve no purpose. At the same time it should be accurate and honest. It must not conceal or gloss over or distort the facts. It should consist essentially of a *Consolidated Balance Sheet* as of the end of the most recent fiscal year, a *Summary Statement of Current Income* and a *Summary Statement of Current Expenditures*—all for the same fiscal year.

If the auditor's financial report is in proper form, it should be possible for the college business office to prepare these statements readily from the report. Better still, once the auditor knows the form that is desired, he can prepare the statements along with his annual financial report. In any event, it is advantageous to have the name of the auditing firm attached in some way to the published financial statement. So, however it is prepared, it should have the auditor's approval.

To avoid any possibility of misunderstanding, let me say a brief word about each of the three parts of this financial statement.

The *Consolidated Balance Sheet* ought to give in condensed and simplified form information that is to be found on one or more balance sheets in the auditor's report. This simplified balance sheet should clearly answer such questions as: What is the total endowment? What is the total value of the plant? What is the total indebtedness and how was it incurred? What is the net worth of the institution? Where figures could be interpreted as book value, market value or replacement value, it should be noted which value is used. In some college financial statements that have come to my attention, the balance sheet has been omitted. It seems to me that a balance sheet is essential in order to give the over-all financial position of the college, showing both assets and liabilities.

The *Summary Statement of Current Income* ought to include all income, with its principal sources, received by the college during the fiscal year just past. It is a condensed version of what appears in the auditor's annual report. In college accounting it is customary to report both income and expenditures under the following main headings: Educational and General; Auxiliary Enterprises; Student Aid. Each main heading has various subheadings which need not be given in the summary statement with as great detail as appears in the annual financial report.

Educational and general income includes all income which the college receives except what is proper to the various auxiliary enterprises and what is intended for student aid or for plant expansion. Since we hear a great deal about the fact that student tuition and other educational fees do not nearly pay the cost of educating the students, it is important to subtotal this student income so that it will stand out clearly. In this way anyone who so wishes may readily compare it with the total "educational and general expenditures."

The *Summary Statement of Current Expenditures* ought to include all the expenditures for the past year, except capital expenditures for such purposes as debt reduction or new building. Like the summary of income, the summary of expenditures is a condensed version of what appears in the auditor's report. The main headings are the same as appear on the income statement, but the subheadings will differ. This is especially true under the major heading "Educational and General." Here the chief subheadings are: "General Administration," which includes the administrative offices, with total salaries of the administrative staff, supplies and miscellaneous expenses, printing, postage and so on; "General Institutional," which includes telephone, interest charges, insurance, membership dues, commencement, concerts, lectures and the like; "Instructional," which covers anything that has to do with the teaching of students, such as salaries of teachers, supplies, and miscellaneous expenses connected with the classroom.

In order that financial statements may be more meaningful, especially for those people who do not like to read figures or who find any financial report confusing, interesting facts and visual representations can be compiled from the income and expenditure statements.

Thus it is possible to state what it cost the college to operate its educational program for the year just past and to indicate what percentage of the cost was borne by students. With the enrollment figure as a divisor, it is possible to show what was the cost per student. A sentence or two will explain from what sources the educational deficit was made up. Another variation in presenting educational income and expense is to show what are the sources in cents of each dollar of income and how each educational dollar is spent—how many cents for instruction, library, administration, general expense, operation of plant, and so forth. All of this, of course, lends itself readily to graphic presentation.

The three parts of this financial statement have been described in some detail because I am convinced of their importance. The adoption of a policy of giving them wide distribution will, I am convinced, repay the college in good public relations. The publication will serve to explain and justify the advances in tuition charges which you have felt compelled to make from time to time. Also it will give your development director a handy factual statement to use as a starting point when soliciting funds from the various constituencies of the college.

I have written to Murchiston College for a copy of their latest financial statement. It follows very closely what I have outlined in this letter. In fact it is my ideal statement. Murchiston has been publishing these statements regularly for the past three years. They are sent to alumni, parents, and friends of the college. Even the students receive them. President Heromy tells me that he is greatly encouraged by the results. I must ask him to send me several copies each year, because I can never hold on very long to the single copy that comes to me. There is always some one who has need for it. As soon as the copy arrives I will forward it to you. I am sure it will help you to interpret what I have written. You may wish to get other samples of published financial reports from college presidents whom you know.

In the meantime, if there are questions in your mind that are not answered in this letter, just pick up the telephone and call me, or drop me a note.

Sincerely,

# 25

## Interinstitutional Cooperation

DEAR PRESIDENT SCHLAGLE:

I have your letter asking my opinion on two different forms of interinstitutional cooperation: a regional grouping of colleges for cooperative action on academic and administrative matters, and a state foundation for joint solicitation of corporate support. I recognize the importance of these questions and I know that they are being asked by a number of college presidents across the country. The basic problem underlying both questions is how far such cooperative enterprises may be expected to benefit the institution for which you are responsible.

As you say, a president can spend a great deal of time helping other people solve their problems while neglecting his own. This is a reaction that one often gets from faculty members and hardheaded trustees. It is commonly said that if the president would spend as much time at home as he does on the road, he would do a better job for the college and probably raise twice as much money into the bargain.

Presidents themselves, of course, have serious doubts about the tangible benefits to be derived from all the meetings they are expected to attend. Some of these meetings, to be sure, are virtually compulsory. A college must usually be represented by its chief executive officer at the principal meetings, at least the annual meetings, of the major national, regional and state organizations to which it belongs. Wisdom dictates, however, that such obligations be kept to the necessary minimum.

At the same time, we must recognize that the president is faced with a perpetual dilemma. Shall he keep his nose so close to the institutional grindstone as to risk the loss of a broad perspective on educational affairs? Or shall he devote time and energy to maintaining informative and stimulating contacts at the expense of his immediate duties? A similar dilemma is raised by cooperative enterprises, but much more is involved, of course, than allocation of the president's time and energy.

Interinstitutional cooperation has been spreading rapidly across the American educational scene in recent years and it has taken many different forms. Some cooperative arrangements are designed for strictly limited purposes, ranging all the way from fund raising through admission procedures to teacher preparation or the provision of non-Western study programs. Such specific arrangements may be either permanent or limited in duration, perhaps to a quite brief experimental period. They vary widely in their geographical scope, from four or five colleges in or near a single city, like the Richmond University Center, to a nationwide organization like the College Entrance Examination Board. Other combinations cover a much wider range, if not the whole gamut, of institutional activities, to the point of constituting what is in effect a federation of colleges. Such an organization necessarily comprises relatively few members, and it is obviously easier to operate if they are located in close proximity to each other. The extreme case, perhaps, is the Claremont group of colleges in California, which is to all intents and purposes a single university composed of constituent colleges, on the Oxford and Cambridge pattern.

Your first question relates particularly, however, to the type of regional cooperation represented by the Associated Colleges of the Midwest and the Great Lakes Colleges Association. Both of these organizations are combinations of liberal arts colleges aimed at increased educational effectiveness and operating economy. They exist solely to help members in their academic purposes, not in fund raising, public relations or matters of public policy. They are rather like universities made up of colleges that are widely separated geographically, except that in this special case the "university" exists purely to strengthen the constituent colleges. In the nature of this form of interinstitutional cooperation, the emphasis is placed on new and experimental areas of action, in which the individual colleges have done, and probably could have done, relatively little on their own account.

Through its Argonne Semester Program, the Associated Colleges of the Midwest has found expensive tools and complex facilities for its students and faculty at the Argonne National Laboratory. It has operated a summer science field-station, faculty seminars and workshops, and a significant experiment in the improvement of language instruction. It has embarked on comparative studies of college and student characteristics, purchased insurance collectively, and sponsored student and faculty conferences on topics of current interest.

Both ACM and GLCA are attempting to find new and creative professional opportunities for their faculties and are becoming extensively engaged in projects of overseas education. Both have plans for Latin American centers, one in Central America and the other in South America, for student instruction and faculty research. The Great Lakes Colleges Association is planning centers in four or five locations representing the major non-Western cultures of the world, as well as corresponding centers, with specialized staff, library resources and language instruction, located at selected member colleges but available to serve them all. It also has a visiting scholars program and a program to clarify and strengthen graduate education among its members and to establish advantageous relations between them and the large graduate schools.

Whether a group of colleges in your own region has sufficient homogeneity and strength to develop and profit from such arrangements, you will have to judge. Before starting a comparable organization, it would be well to ask: What is there in common among the colleges concerned? Are they all equally autonomous? Is each one of them capable of taking part in cooperative enterprises while preserving its unique character? In the Midwest group a high degree of homogeneity and considerable experience of working together clearly existed. All were liberal arts colleges of roughly the same size; all independent or church-related; all engaged mainly in the teaching of undergraduates; all more or less similar in financial structure. Likewise, the Great Lakes group, in the words of its president, had in common "regional proximity, private support, liberal arts emphasis, high academic standards, and above all now, a desire to work together for experiment and improvement."

If all or most of these conditions are fulfilled, and if the participating colleges are serious enough about the enterprise to put up money for a small but dynamic central office, including salary and travel expenses for a first-rate executive officer, the range of potential benefits is almost unlimited. They include economies of size, strength in negotiation and complementary specialization. The strengths of each college can be exploited and its weaknesses remedied to an extent that is virtually impossible if each college stands alone. Working together fosters the kind of collective judgment and mutual inspiration that cannot be duplicated on individual campuses. Through joint planning and pooled resources, broader research projects can be developed; enlarged opportunities can be offered to students to prepare themselves for a swiftly changing society; a healthy spirit of professional competition can be aroused; a higher quality of faculty and students may be attracted; and foundations and individual benefactors may be encouraged to invest in projects that are of more than institutional significance.

For my own part, I am convinced that close intercollegiate cooperation offers the most promising remedy for what has always been one of the worst weaknesses of small liberal arts colleges and threatens to be a still more serious handicap to the vast majority of them in the years that lie ahead. I mean their relative remoteness from the "growing edge" of knowledge. However it may have been in the past, the future holds little promise for a college that cannot attract teachers who are active scholars and students who seek the inspiration of such teachers. But to provide the facilities needed for active scholarship, and I don't mean only research equipment for the natural sciences, is beyond the reach of all but a tiny minority of our undergraduate colleges, if they are to operate as completely self-contained units. I believe, therefore, that in the immediate future we may expect to see a number of other organizations like ACM and GLCA come into being. But every college must decide for itself whether the job it aspires to do can be done better by going it alone or in partnership with others.

Your second question refers to cooperative fund raising through state foundations. I am particularly glad to discuss this with you, as I have had long experience of the movement.

First, you must realize that this type of collaboration is open to much the same criticism as any other cooperative activity. Faculty and trustees often think that a president could raise more money if he were to concentrate his efforts on his own institution rather than seek funds for a group of colleges. At the beginning of the state foundation movement, this was one of the most persistent objections that had to be met.

On the basis of experience, however, the reverse turned out to be true. Industrialists, while sometimes wishing to designate their gifts for particular colleges, tended to be deeply impressed by a joint visit from two college presidents representing a whole group of institutions. They were especially gratified when they found that the pair represented different religious denominations. It was sometimes quite a shock for them to see a Roman Catholic nun and a Protestant minister walk in together.

While all state associations have not been equally effective, they have on the whole been successful in arousing public interest in the financial problems of private colleges. Joint solicitation is not merely a means of raising money but also an opportunity of achieving better understanding between higher education and the business world. Many topics of common concern—economic development, population changes, automation, governmental policies, the increasing need for college graduates to man industry—may come up for discussion in interviews between college presidents and businessmen. Nobody can tell, of course, just how much the state foundation movement has influenced the growth of corporate support for higher education, but support from both large and small corporations is certainly growing.

In fund-raising activities, as in other phases of cooperation, there are the drawbacks we have noted. The chief difficulty for college presidents is the scheduling of sufficient time, usually the equivalent of two or three weeks a year, to accomplish the job. Experience has shown that this work cannot be delegated to other officers without loss of effectiveness. Yet a disciplined use of time can enable the president to fulfill his first and most important role as educator. In all aspects of cooperation, care must be exercised not to become overwhelmed with engagements or frustrated with inconsequential activity. Fund raising, in particular, must be kept in proper relationship with the fundamental aims of the college.

My advice, then, President Schlagle, is not to shut the door to cooperation, but to be cautious about accepting engagements that will not directly benefit, either immediately or in the foreseeable future, the college for which you are responsible. In determining what you yourself should and should not do, you of course, are the best judge. Don't spread yourself too thin!

With hearty good wishes, I am

Sincerely,

# 26

## The President's Intellectual Life

DEAR PRESIDENT HOSMER:

I have great sympathy for your statement that you have almost no time for scholarly study in your new post. I know
exactly how you feel. I have found that most other college presidents are struggling with the same problem.

You ask if there is any way in which you could adjust your
administrative responsibilities so that you would have regular
times for study and writing. It may not be very comforting to
know that this question is perhaps more frequently asked than
any other that comes to me, and I feel less competent to answer
it. But I shall try to share with you my own experience and that
of other college administrators with whom I have discussed
the matter.

Everybody recognizes that scholarship is the main business of
a college and that a president would increase his stature with
his faculty and the academic community if he could carry on at
least a minimum of scholarly endeavor. In a few of the older,
well-established institutions, it seems more possible to do this.
The staff is larger and is accustomed to carrying responsibilities
that must be borne by the president in a smaller school. There
are presidents of small colleges, however, who have succeeded
in reserving sufficient time for study and writing to be able to
get out an occasional scholarly paper, a magazine article or a
chapter in a book. There is no question that almost all college
administrators would like to do this kind of thing. At any rate,

they aspire to keep up their scholarship, even though frustrated by the emergencies that continually arise.

No matter how heavy a president's load, or how large or small the institution with which he is connected, given adequate will power, he can find a way for some systematic study and writing. Thereby he can at least maintain his intellectual self-respect and a feeling of identity with the scholarly fraternity. Even if the odds are at times overwhelming, it is important to keep on trying.

I have observed that those who seem to make most headway with programs of study and writing reserve periods of isolation at summer or winter study cabins, or arrange with a local hotel to hide away occasionally from telephones, colleagues and visitors. A wise secretary can be extremely helpful in protecting the president from unnecessary interruptions. With careful planning and the cooperation of staff associates, a few presidents have carried on first-class studies and have maintained their stature as active participants in a learned society. A president can employ assistants in gathering data which he can check and write up in his spare moments. When sufficient material has been gathered, he can take a brief winter or summer holiday and bring together his findings in a series of articles or a book.

President Bowman of Johns Hopkins University told a group of educators that a college president can and must keep up his scholarship. A president, he continued, needs to be known for some academic achievement as well as his administrative skill. While it is not easy to arrange for adequate study time, President Bowman concluded, those who are determined to do so can find time to read while en route to and from educational conferences, while sitting in an airport or railway station, or taking an extra day in a hotel after fulfilling an engagement. President Wriston tells us that he insisted at both Lawrence and Brown on budgeting a period each week when he could put aside his administrative duties and turn with uninterrupted joy to the kind of reading and writing that had meant so much to him during his years as a teacher.

Apart from their intrinsic value, study projects unrelated to administrative problems can be both broadening and refreshing. They encourage fresh thinking, open-mindedness, objectivity and a disciplined use of time—all of which are valuable in the general administration of the institution.

In my own case, I found that expanding an old master's thesis and reworking material for a doctor's dissertation was useful in helping understand liberal learning against a background of contemporary problems. It helped me in redefining the college purpose, conferring with faculty members on curricular matters and working out a long-term plan for development of the institution. These studies also provided me with release and gave me a sense of relaxation when the going was hard.

Other presidents have related similar experiences and have said that wrestling with a problem in nuclear physics, finding more effective ways of getting food to underdeveloped countries, dealing with a knotty problem in international law, reviewing a novel or assisting in a new approach to the teaching of chemistry have given them perspective, clarified their thinking and gained respect from their faculty associates.

But scholarship does not have to be confined to subjects unrelated to the administrative responsibilities of a president. New theories of education are being published continually, and should be checked against the experience and point of view of a given institution. One of the great advantages of American higher education is its variety; and the individuality of presidents and institutions should provide a fresh source of experimentation and reflection. The care with which a study is planned and the way in which it is carried out can evoke both admiration and cooperation from faculty members and students. Such an example can even stimulate independent study, interdepartmental research and college-community learning projects.

I hardly need to say that there is a danger of getting swamped by trying to read too much of the literature on higher education that piles up on one's desk or nearby bookshelves. Along with this goes the danger of limiting oneself to this kind of reading. Time must be found for some solid reading, unrelated to the president's administrative tasks, if he is to stay intellectually alive, if he is to keep growing as a person. (I have never forgotten the remark I once heard made by a distinguished university professor: "I am sorry for college presidents. They are all intellectually dead.")

I go a bit further. I think that at least a modicum of "escape reading" is highly advisable in the interest of sanity and relief from pressure and tension. Much of this kind of literature may well be trivial and ephemeral. On the other hand there is much of beauty, of charm, and of superb use of the English language to be discovered in books in which the reader can lose himself without being taxed to intellectual exertion.

Now I venture one additional suggestion which may seem somewhat irrelevant but which, in my judgment, is important. There are times when, in the midst of the busiest days, the president is well advised to turn his back on his desk, piled however high with reports and correspondence; ignore his bookshelves loaded with new volumes that he *should* read; look out of the most convenient window—and *think;* or, perhaps, just sit and gaze and turn his mind loose. If this means indulging in revery, even if it means a bit of dozing, still it is *not* time wasted.

Such brief interludes do not need to be planned for or scheduled—indeed they hardly *can* be. Vacations, holidays, scheduled times for rest, for recreation, for play, are essential. What is suggested here is something quite different: it is release, even if no more than momentary, right in the midst of the pressures and tensions of responsibility for making decisions and "getting things done." The art of "turning loose" briefly when the pressures are actually most insistent is, as many can testify, a most rewarding one, though not easily mastered. Often one can turn back to desk or bookstand or conference table with a new surge of energy. And sometimes such brief periods of release provide —who can say whence they come?—new ideas, new insights, new inspiration. One does not have to be, even at the most demanding times, frenetically busy in order to assure oneself and to demonstrate to others that one is "on the job."

Of course we have to face the fact that for most of us there is a virtually inescapable conflict between true scholarship and the day-to-day routine of executive action. Unhurried exploration of ideas, re-examination of them, experimenting with them, writing about them, call for time and for uninterrupted, attentive effort. Only rare individuals can turn quickly and effectively from research and writing to decision-making and back again. The hum of conversation, telephone calls, lines of people waiting for interviews, the endless succession of committees and conferences are diametrically opposed to the demands of first-class scholarship.

On the other hand, reading, writing, composing and other forms of creative activity—if only the president will make time for them—will give him relief from some of the criticisms that inevitably come. At such times, misunderstanding and frustration can be overcome by seeking solace in the great ideas that have shaped man's destiny. When it is impossible to go to one's colleagues, board members or others for comfort or advice, the president may "walk his lonesome valley" with the great minds and spirits found in the Bible and other enduring literature.

With this in mind, may I urge you, President Hosmer, never to let your thirst for knowledge and your devotion to learning lag. This ideal is not easy to achieve, I admit, but as we were not given "a spirit of timidity, but a spirit of power, of love and of self-control," I am confident that you can rise above both criticism and adulation in maintaining the scholarly excellence for which you and your institution are well known.

As you see, I am strongly committed to such a course of action, but I didn't expect that it would take an entire letter to tell you so.

Sincerely,

# 27

## *Home Life—If Any*

Dear President Newcomer:

First, allow me to thank you and your wife for the hospitality of your charming home.

My wife and I were particularly interested in your questions about the use of the president's house; time spent with the family; recreation, sabbaticals and compensation. There is no doubt that these are vital questions which concern almost every college executive. Obviously the problems vary with colleges and people and have to be answered in the light of individual situations.

Summarizing the impressions we exchanged with reference to these questions, I know you agree that the president's home and family are basic to his success as an administrator. This is conspicuously true of the small, church-related or independent college, but it is scarcely less important for the presidents of large city or state universities. In such institutions, although it is often more difficult for the president to have guests in his home, or to bring his family into touch with faculty members and students, when he does so there is an evident growth in respect and friendliness that can mean much to the institution.

The importance of maintaining this kind of administration-faculty-student relationship is such that most colleges, large or small, undertake to provide their presidents with commodious houses. These are generally sufficient not only for the housing of the family but for the entertainment of special guests, faculty dinner parties, and meetings with students. Sometimes they are so elaborate as to provoke murmurs that the funds thus invested might have been better used to provide improved teaching facilities or to give greater financial stability to the college.

One president's wife told me that she was deeply wounded when a professor made a remark of this kind about the president's house that the college was building. But her resentment was happily overcome when the professor became a vocal admirer of the family spirit which he admitted had been brought to the campus by the new home. We have generally found that, where the president's home is open to faculty members, students and alumni, the community is enthusiastic about the situation. People appreciate a place of dignity and beauty around which the social life of the college can revolve. Ideally, the president's house should be a model of taste and friendliness for the entire campus.

Being sensitive to criticism and fearing charges of extravagance, some presidents have insisted on owning their own houses. In some cases they are little more than cottages. Whatever the size, experience has shown that, if properly used, the president's home can make an effective contribution to campus life. If the house is small, of course, most entertaining has to be done in a college dining-room or guest house, under a hostess and the director of the food service. At such times the president's wife works with the appropriate people in determining, according to the nature of the occasion, the menu, the seating arrangement and the conduct of the reception that precedes or follows.

In some cases the president makes his home in a hotel, a downtown apartment or some other place remote from the campus. In urban universities this may be all that is possible. Where this occurs, some other officer of the college usually undertakes to supply the family atmosphere. In such circumstances, as I have already suggested, the president and his wife should try to be available and share in the college fellowship. There is no one who can take their places. People want to know them and to feel that they are interested in the concerns and achievements of the faculty, the students and the community.

The second problem we talked about had to do with the time the president spends with his family. I know how concerned you are about this matter—as indeed you should be.

In at least one presidential family that I know, the children felt that their house was little more than a hotel. The continuous coming and going of visitors, many of whom were well-known people of various races and nationalities, meant little to the children. They noted the difference between their home and those of their playmates, and felt that in some way they were always on parade. Worse still, they felt robbed of the undivided interest of their father and mother. It was a bit of a shock when one day the eldest boy said: "Dad, please get out your book. I want to make an appointment." He had decided that this was the only way he could get his father's attention.

I must confess from my own experience that, even on occasions when my wife and I had made a special effort to reserve time for our children, unexpected visitors, telephone calls and college emergencies often caused the family to feel left out or of secondary importance.

There are, of course, compensations that may not become apparent until later in life. When the children are grown up, they will probably look back with gratitude on their childhood experiences in a president's home. They will realize that meeting famous and unusual people, hearing stories of far-away lands and listening over the breakfast or dinner table to half-understood conversations about the world's problems helped to awaken their curiosity and enlarge their understanding.

But, with all this, any man who has to combine the demanding role of a college president with the raising of a family will have a constant struggle to strike a balance between his competing responsibilities.

As I recall how hard I had to fight to have a genuine home life, I would strongly encourage you to reserve definite afternoons, evenings or weekends for your family and not let *anything*, including important visitors, interfere.

A good way to do this is to leave town from time to time. Rent or buy a place of retreat, a cabin or shack, not many miles from the campus but far enough away so that your secretary can say you are "out of town." Also arrange camping trips, on which swimming, fishing, a building project, or just plain hiking will help you to know the members of the family as individuals and provide an opportunity for comradeship such as few other experiences can give. Long auto trips, picnics and holiday excursions may also help. I would recommend holding regular family councils at which any member of the family, young or old, may bring up a question or express a point of view that will be respected and given full consideration by the rest of the family. One president told me that this family council had done more than anything else to keep him humble and provide a right perspective for his work.

A third problem we discussed was recreation. Remembering my own experience and that of other presidents I have talked with, I am convinced that there is no substitute for the healthy, balanced outlook that grows out of and is sustained by an ample supply of physical and mental energy. One outburst of temper, one unfortunate decision made under stress of overwork, may undo months of constructive effort. To maintain the vigor and elasticity needed for the job requires a definite, systematic and unbreakable program of recreation. It should include a few minutes of daily exercise and an hour or two a week of strenuous play in the gymnasium, on the tennis court, in the swimming pool or wherever it may be. Incidentally, such activities are not only essential to a president's physical and mental health but they offer opportunities for cultivating friendly relations with faculty members, students and administrative colleagues. In addition to regular physical exercise, the president should, as a matter of course, take summer and winter vacations with his family.

I realize that this may sound like a counsel of perfection; that it is far from easy to find time for an adequate recreational program. In fact, it is an occupational disease of the conscientious administrator to make the mistake of sacrificing his personal fitness to duties that could safely be deferred or delegated to subordinates. There may be times when you will have to turn to your wife and your trustees to fortify your resolution and still your qualms of conscience. You will be unluckier than most

presidents I know if they are not happy to do so—not just out
of personal concern for you but from sober recognition of
the paramount importance of your health and equanimity to the
continuing welfare of the college. Indeed I should expect the
board, no less than your wife, to give wholehearted support to
your establishing a definite schedule of annual vacations.

A president of my acquaintance learned an unforgettable
lesson when his wife went ahead on her own and paid the rent
in advance on a cottage in the mountains for a six weeks' vacation. At first the idea seemed preposterous. The president was
facing an unusually difficult financial situation; faculty problems were weighing on him; community relations were giving
trouble; burgeoning opportunities demanded his continuous
attention. Under these conditions, to go completely away for
so long a period was manifestly unthinkable (a little reflection
would have shown him that it always would be).

As soon as the proposal got noised abroad, however, teachers
and administrative colleagues joined in urging the president to
go. A division of labor was worked out; the duties he would
normally have performed were assigned to the appropriate officers; the president's secretary was instructed that no official
papers were to be sent on to him and nothing was to be referred
to him by telephone or telegraph except in case of absolute
necessity. Why not? If he had fallen sick and been laid up for
six weeks, some such arrangements would have had to be made
perforce. My friend told me afterwards that he had had a wonderful summer, and his family was tied together as never before. At the same time, he achieved a new perspective on college
problems and policies, which was of benefit for years afterwards.
And, wonder of wonders! the college administration itself was
reinvigorated; a team spirit developed and a new plateau of
effectiveness was reached.

There is a lesson here for the "indispensable" chief executive.

Yet a fourth problem we considered was that of sabbaticals
and salaries as they relate to the president.

Although I never had a sabbatical, and few presidents do, I
agree with you that there is no reason why the president should
not have one just like any other member of the faculty. With a

well-trained executive staff and a strong board chairman, it should be possible for the president to take a leave of absence every seven years. The fresh perspective and renewed energy which a sabbatical will provide should more than make up for any inconvenience caused by his absence and, on balance, provide a great profit for the college.

Again, there is the matter of compensation for the president. This is a subject which most college administrators are reluctant to discuss, and yet they know it must have attention. In my visits to colleges, it has not been unusual for me to find presidents facing real hardship. Even though they know they are commonly supposed to receive twice the salary of the highest paid professor, they rarely do. The chairman of the board of trustees, if nobody else, ought to keep the president's remuneration in mind. Naturally, a dedicated president who, in the last analysis, is responsible both for the solvency of the college and for the salaries of everyone else, will hesitate to do anything about his own. He may argue that he is better cared for than most of his colleagues, that he can wait until the college is in a better position to raise salaries all around.

While this may be true, it must be remembered that college presidents have no security. They are not on tenure and they are vulnerable to attacks that have little to do with their administrative competence or the quality of their leadership. Moreover, college administration is so specialized that it may not be easy for a president to find a new post if he is driven to resign.

It is also often overlooked that the president, by virtue of his office, is under an obligation to contribute substantially to community causes, to pay membership dues to a variety of organizations, to absorb some of the overhead of a heavy travel program, and in some cases to assist in the social and religious activities of the denomination with which his college is affiliated. It is therefore important that a president's salary be sufficient for him to meet these obligations, while making adequate provision for his children's education and the purchase of a retirement home. Without this, some presidents, who have done excellent work and are widely appreciated, have been forced, upon retirement, to find other income or be cared for by their relatives.

In summary, my advice, based on my own experience and observations, is that a president, while giving complete dedication to the college, must not neglect his responsibility to himself and his family. It is wise to make full use of one's home both as a retreat and as a center of family atmosphere for the institution, but this must not interfere with the bringing up of children or with the vacations and family projects necessary to a happy and wholesome family life. Recreation, including adequate periods of complete relaxation away from campus, is essential, and sabbaticals and sufficient compensation must be assured by an alert and imaginative chairman of the board of trustees or by some other officer specifically charged with the responsibility. To pay due attention to these things is not a matter of self-interest but part of the duty that the president owes to his college.

Again, thank you for a wonderful visit, and please keep me in touch.

Sincerely,

# 28

## To a President's Wife

DEAR MRS. NEWCOMER:

My husband has passed on to me your request for advice on how to tackle the unfamiliar role of a college president's wife. I guess he thought that a woman who had played the part for half a lifetime was in the best position to respond. And certainly, after a good many years in a president's home, plus visits to quite a number of others, I have probably seen examples of most kinds of problems you are likely to encounter.

First of all, let me tell you candidly that the life of the president's wife is not an easy one. You may reply that this is true of most wives and mothers. But being married to a college president entails problems over and above the usual vicissitudes of married life. The president's wife is in a different situation from that of the wife of any other professional man, except perhaps a clergyman.

This is because of the nature of the president's task. It is not the kind of job that a man goes to in the morning and comes away from at night (even if he sometimes brings home a loaded briefcase). The college president never leaves his job behind, except on annual vacation and an occasional weekend—if he is wise enough to insist on such necessary breaks—and even then he is apt to be followed by long-distance calls. Not only does he carry greater personal responsibility than most public servants or business executives, but he is more than a mere administrator: he is the head of a kind of outsize family. More often than

not, his home is on or close to the campus. So he is at everybody's beck and call throughout his waking hours, and they tend
to be quite a large fraction of the twenty-four.

The president's wife can hardly escape corresponding obligations. She is not plain Mrs. X but "Mrs. President"—first lady
of an academic community and probably also a fairly prominent
figure in a larger social environment. Like her husband, she is
always on parade.

I disagree with what was once said to me by a college consultant of wide experience, when trying to reassure me at a low
point in my feelings of usefulness: "Don't worry. The college
will get by. Some institutions are quite well managed when
there is no wife in the picture at all." Not very flattering or encouraging! But, right or wrong, the observation is scarcely helpful to a woman who is the wife of a president. She presumably
wants to help her husband as much as she can, and in most
colleges I know of she is far from being expected not to worry
about college affairs.

If not exactly married to the job as well as the man, she can
hardly help being a kind of unpaid college officer. If she cares
about her husband's career and his college, she will be both a
mother and a model to the academic family (in competition
with her own!), and, like most mothers and models, pretty much
of a target too. Her home will certainly not be her castle, and
she cannot expect anything like the private life that most
middle-class women take for granted.

So it is a hard row to hoe for a woman who sets a high value
on personal privacy, who wants "to live her own life in her own
way," who does not care for too many social engagements and
expects her husband to give a generous share of his attention
to his family. Even for a couple with the outgoing temperament
that the position demands, it is a constant struggle to strike a
fair balance between public duties and domestic responsibilities.

For the career woman the difficulties are compounded. I
should hate to suggest that a college president should not be
married to a wife with a career of her own. The college presidency requires an unusual combination of intellectual and
moral qualities. The kind of man one likes to see in the post is

apt to marry the same kind of woman, and that kind of woman may well have established herself in a professional career. It would be too bad if this were a bar to her husband's taking a job for which he is eminently suited.

But it is no use blinking the difficulties. The career woman, as I have seen her, usually has a full-time job in town, with her own professional associates and obligations. She is often on boards or committees of national or regional organizations, and may have to fly off periodically to New York or Chicago or wherever it may be. Obviously she cannot give much time to campus problems or be bothered with much entertaining. I remember going with my husband on an official visit to a college where the president's wife was in this position. We found that she was out of town and apparently did not know of our coming. Her maid had not been told that guests were expected. This kind of experience inevitably leaves a poor impression on visitors. They cannot help feeling that something is missing.

Even for wives like you, who do not have this special problem, there are many pitfalls.

A sympathetic and tactful "Mrs. President" can be a help to the college staff. The buildings and grounds department, for instance, may welcome her advice on landscaping, decoration and furnishing—or, of course, they may not. Deans of students in a small college may find her an invaluable helper. But she has to be constantly on her guard lest she overstep the mark and become a tiresome busybody. Of course, she is not the only campus wife who can make a nuisance of herself, but she is particularly conspicuous if she does.

Nothing is more disruptive of campus harmony than a president's wife with inflated ideas of her social status. Her attitude toward the college family is that of a feudal lady. She thinks that faculty wives are somehow responsible to her and that their time is at her disposal. This attitude may extend to the superintendent of buildings and grounds, the business manager and even faculty members. Need I tell you that such a situation may give rise to deep resentment and create serious administrative problems? I know of one case in which the board of trustees had to ask the lady in question to refrain from such behavior, even though in doing so they risked the resignation of her husband.

A mother's natural feeling that her first duty is to her children may lead her unintentionally to let the children rule the roost to the extent of becoming campus pests. And the peculiar situation of the president's family—like ministers' and missionaries' children—is fraught with danger for the children themselves. They are likely to get both too little attention and too much. Sometimes they are teased, or are allowed too many privileges by faculty and students. Giving one's children a healthy and sensible upbringing in these conditions is quite a special problem. Occasionally a president has even felt obliged to resign his post in order to be able to rear his family in a less trying environment.

The president's wife may find tightrope walking equally necessary in the care and feeding of her husband. It follows from the nature of the position that the president's wife can be either a great help to him in bearing his exacting burdens, or a great handicap. One of her hardest tasks is simply keeping the man in good health. She may have to plan a vacation over his protests and pay rent on a cottage in advance, or something of that kind, in order to force him to take a needed rest. At home, she can protect him from unnecessary interviews by listening politely to callers and simply promising to inform him. Occasionally she may be able to take his place at social functions. But she can cause misunderstanding and gossip if she lets her concern for her husband's welfare drive her into a defensive attitude that betrays resentment of the demands made upon him, let alone on herself.

Sometimes, a sense of the intolerable burdens of the presidential office may inspire in a sensitive woman a feeling of her own inadequacy for helping her husband and playing her own part in college affairs. She may be tempted to withdraw from campus activities and hide behind closed doors and drawn shades. Goodness knows, such a reaction is understandable, but it never helps and is easily misunderstood.

Yes, there are plenty of pitfalls, but for a person like you the way to avoid them is to be yourself and try to keep your job in perspective. Don't exaggerate your responsibilities or let them get you down. If you keep a cool head and a sense of humor, you can make a contribution to the welfare of the college that can be made by nobody else, and you will find satisfactions such as few other women enjoy.

You will be mixing, day by day, with expectionally intelligent and interesting men and women. Faculty members and their wives will, as a rule, be delighted to help you carry out your social responsibilities and to aid in putting on such special college celebrations as Homecoming, Commencement and Alumni Day. Besides this, your home may be a center of stimulating contacts with guests from all over the world. You will always be glad to remember that you entertained the prime minister of Pakistan, or Marian Anderson, or the Juilliard String Quartet. Other pleasures and satisfactions will come from cultural contacts on campus or in the local community. You will find that your position as the president's wife gives you entry into any group you care to give time to. In fact, you will have to make rules for yourself and pick and choose carefully among the many opportunities for combining service with enjoyment, so as not to run yourself ragged with endless engagements.

It goes without saying that, as official hostess, the president's wife is responsible for helping plan and give parties, large or small, and for introducing faculty members to visitors and guests. She can also help trustees and townspeople to appreciate the college, as well as assist students and faculty to develop a feeling of mutual confidence and family relationship. In this role, she must realize how easily she can wear herself out physically. She should, if necessary, be quite firm with her husband and the trustees in asking to be provided with a home and equipment ample for official entertaining, and to be given an allowance sufficient to provide at least part-time regular help.

The social education of students, both boys and girls, can be facilitated by their experience as guests in the president's home. Informal parties are needed, yes, but also the knowledge of how to seat a lady at table, to rise when she enters the room, to help with wraps, open doors, and so forth. Social courtesies, well learned, detract nothing from a *magna cum laude*.

The president's wife must be an example of taste and simplicity in entertaining. An elaborate dinner of many courses, served by a maid, may be something to talk about, but few faculty wives are likely to be able to do the same. And dissatisfaction and even jealousy may result if the president's entertaining is too lavish. Simplicity on the part of the president's wife is also important in the matter of dress. It is her duty always to dress attractively and on special occasions to "dress up" because she is both representing the college and setting a standard for it. Extravagant and expensive clothing, however, is to be avoided, as are extreme sports clothes and negligées. One never knows who will next ring the doorbell.

Moreover, a president's wife's social affairs should be well planned. On such occasions a group of faculty wives should be asked to help with introductions, pouring tea and taking wraps. Generally such requests are considered a compliment, and people like being part of the festivities. Care should be exercised, however, to extend invitations so that no one group seems to be favored.

This does not mean, of course, that the president's wife cannot have her own personal friends, or that she should not try to create an environment that will encourage campus wives to drop in for a call or "come over" to see if there is anything they can help with. The important thing is that she should not give any ground for suspicion that she is the center of a clique that enjoys some kind of special relationship with the administration. Even with her closest friends, she must observe reasonable discretion in talking about college affairs.

No matter how congenial and intimate the relationship may be, there are always a few people who try to advance their own or their husband's position by getting at the president through his wife. To them a promotion or raise is so patently deserved that they think it would not be at all out of place for the president's wife to intercede for them. She must be on her guard, however, and make some such reply as: "Your husband had better talk to the head of his department or the president himself. We make it a rule never to discuss such matters in the family." The word soon gets around that the president's wife cannot be used in this manner, and there is general satisfaction.

Often professors, too, try to get the jump on the rest of the faculty by finding out administrative or board decisions before they are made public. They often ask point blank some such a question as: "Where is the new library to be built?" and have to be answered: "If a decision has been reached, I have not heard it announced." That's that!

One thing is sure: a college president's wife has no excuse for feeling that "the one at the top is always lonely." She has a large official family, any of whose members she may visit, if she wishes, or invite for an evening at her home. And if she meets every day's situation with determination to do her part, she will find that she is having an exciting and fascinating life.

So, along with my best wishes for success in your new life, I offer you my hearty congratulations on a wonderful opportunity.

Sincerely,

# Bibliography

To read everything that gets into print in this field is obviously impossible for any one person. The president is compelled to be selective. Most of the printed material that comes to his desk can be glanced at, passed on to one or another of his associates or, in at least some instances, consigned to the waste-basket. The president is fortunate who has cultivated the art of rapid reading and evaluation. He is fortunate, too, if he has managed to reserve time for the careful reading of those publications that seem to merit such attention. In the selective process he can sometimes be helped by a competent assistant or secretary who is able to digest or summarize some of the printed material and provide suggestions as to what merits further attention by the president.

The selected, briefly annotated bibliography which follows is intended to be suggestive only. It will be noted that all the books here listed have been published within the last ten years—about half of them in 1960 or later. Many of these books will provide an abundance of additional references on specific topics, and much more extensive bibliographies are available.

AYERS, ARCHIE R., and RUSSEL, JOHN H., *Internal Structure; Organization and Administration of Institutions of Higher Education,* Bulletin 1962, No. 9, U.S. Department of Health, Education, and Welfare, Washington, 1962, 123 + vii pages

A systematic report on the administrative organization of institutions of higher education, based on a study of the patterns of 608 colleges and universities: designed to provide "guidelines for evaluation and modification." Four major areas of administrative responsibility are recognized. There are detailed "job specifications," some 30 pages of statistical tables, and commentary on the interrelationships of the administrative offices and on alternative patterns. Does not invite "straightaway" reading, but will be a useful reference book on numerous specific questions.

BRUBACHER, JOHN S., and RUDY, WILLIS, *Higher Education in Transition —an American History: 1636-1956,* Harper and Brothers, New York, 1958, 494 pages

A scholarly review, from colonial beginnings, of the development of higher education in the United States; intended to provide historical perspective for meeting the problems of higher education of the future. Part IV, *Higher Education in the Twentieth Century* (pages 233-369), includes a chapter on *The Enlarging Scope of the Administration of Higher Education*. Part V (pages 373-390) summarizes *Distinguishing Features of American Higher Education*. This final chapter is followed by 88 pages of consolidated footnotes.

BRUMBAUGH, A. J., *Problems in College Administration,* Board of Education, The Methodist Church, Nashville, 1956, 50 pages

A compact, well organized, practical discussion, with much of wisdom and common sense packed into it. Neither exhaustive nor exhausting, it is good first reading for the novice president. A brief bibliography includes publications between 1932 and 1955.

BURNS, GERALD P., Editor, *Administrators in Higher Education: Their Functions and Coordination,* Harper and Brothers, New York, 1962, 236 pages

Fifteen different authors contribute the introduction and the fourteen chapters dealing with various aspects of academic administration. The first four chapters are general in character; Chapter 5 deals with the trustees or regents; there follow 8 chapters treating of the major administrative officers, with a final chapter of summary and evaluation. While the administrative charts and much of the discussion are most applicable to larger, complex institutions, there is much of suggestion for the administrator of the small college. Specially commended for careful analysis and interpretation are the chapters (9 through 12) dealing with student personnel work, public relations, development, admissions and record-keeping.

CORSON, JOHN J., *Governance of Colleges and Universities,* McGraw-Hill Book Company, Inc., New York, 1960, 209 pages

Based on first-hand observation of the functioning of ten institutions and on conversation and correspondence with many trustees, presidents, deans and teachers. Much of the discussion relates chiefly to the university. Of particular interest to the presidents of small colleges may be the final two of the eight chapters: *The Ecology of Governance* and *Institutional Character and Leadership.* An appendix of fifteen pages provides helpful *Comments on Selected Readings.*

DODDS, HAROLD W., *The Academic President: Educator or Caretaker?* McGraw-Hill Book Company, Inc., New York, 1962, 294 + ix pages

This book is the outcome of an extensive study financed by the Carnegie Corporation of New York and the Carnegie Foundation for the Advancement of Teaching. The author and two collaborators visited "approximately sixty colleges and universities." A "number of representative universities" were selected for "intensive team study." Interviews were conducted with "presidents, trustees, academic vice-presidents, deans, non-academic officers of administration, members of the faculty of all ranks, and students." The discussions range widely, with much of variant and alternative suggestion, and the reader may wish at times that conclusions and recommendations were brought into sharper focus. While chiefly concerned with the universities where "the problems are most apparent and most acute," there is much that will be of interest and value to presidents of liberal arts colleges. There is concern for the preservation of the "historic, essential nature" of the presidency, i.e., for the president's role as an educational leader; there is emphasis also upon the need for mastery of the "art of administration"—which, in itself, implies much more than being a "caretaker." The answer to the question in the sub-title would seem to be "both." Full of practical hints are Chapter III on *The President and the Art of Administration* and subsequent sections on *The Place of Deans in Academic Government; Academic Planning; Public Relations; The President and the Chairman of the Board;* and *The Apprenticeship Approach to Administration.*

DRESSEL, PAUL L. and ASSOCIATES, *Evaluation in Higher Education,* Houghton Mifflin Company, Boston, 1961, 480 + xvi pages

Ten "associates" contribute to the volume in addition to the senior author and editor. Interpreting evaluation broadly, this is a highly competent critical discussion, of value chiefly to the specialist in this field, but it should also be of interest to the administrator who realizes that evaluation of variant types is involved in many phases of administrative procedure and planning. There are six chapters on the general nature of evaluation and its relationship to instruction and learning (1, 2, 3, 8, 9 and 11); four on evaluation in specific subject-matter fields (4, 5, 6 and 7); one on selection, classification and placement of students (10); two on institutional self-studies and regional (or state) surveys (12 and 13). Each chapter is followed by *Suggestions for Further Reading.* While highly specialized discussions, each chapter provides suggested implications for higher education that range beyond the merely technical. Two appendices deal with techniques of measurement and provide an illustrative outline for a state-wide survey.

EDDY, EDWARD D. JR., *The College Influence on Student Character,* American Council on Education, Washington, 1959, 185 + xii pages

A report of an exploratory study sponsored by the American Council on Education through its Committee for Study of Character Development in Education. The author, with two assistants, visited twenty American colleges and universities, employing the "participant-observer approach," supplemented by "formal, open-ended interviews with both students and members of the faculty." In the first chapter the assumptions guiding the study are clearly stated, the basic one being "that among its responsibilities the American college should include a conscious concern for the character of its students." Chapter 2, *The Level of Expectancy,* sets the tone and presents the challenge which is elaborated in subsequent chapters. The final chapter, *The Possible and the Potential,* includes a section on *Areas for Exploration.* Much importance is attached to expressions of student opinion, with little critical evaluation of such expressions. No claims are made as to the "scientific" character of the study. Thus, unburdened with statistics, the book is frankly impressionistic and invites the reader's own appraisal of the validity of the conclusions reached.

GARDNER, JOHN W., *Excellence, Can We be Equal and Excellent Too?*
  Harper and Brothers, New York, 1961, 171 + xiv pages

A challenging, wise and highly readable discussion of the ideal of excellence in relationship to democratic concepts of equality. Part II, *Talent,* and Part III, *Individual Differences,* have direct bearing on education. Especially to be noted are Chapter VII, *Education as a Sorting Out Process, and Chapter VIII, College and the Alternatives.* In the second of these two chapters the whole argument comes into sharp focus in unforgettable paragraphs (pages 85-86) beginning: "In short we reject the notion that excellence is something that can only be experienced in the most rarified strata of higher education . . . we must *demand* it everywhere. We must ask for excellence in every form which higher education takes." Stimulating, rewarding reading throughout.

HENDERSON, ALGO D., *Policies and Practices in Higher Education,* Harper
  and Brothers, New York, 1960, 338 pages.

A comprehensive review of current issues and trends in American higher education. The table of contents is so organized as to make it easy for the reader to turn to discussion of any topic of particular immediate interest. Part V (pages 217-297) is devoted to *Administration.* The final chapter, constituting Part VI (pages 301-321), discusses *Strengths and Weaknesses of American Higher Education.* There are *Selected References,* grouped by sections (pages 323-330), in addition to footnotes in each chapter.

HOFSTADTER, RICHARD, and SMITH, WILSON, *American Higher Education
  —A Documentary History,* University of Chicago Press, Chicago, 1961,
  2 volumes, 1016 pages

Selected documents illustrating the problems faced by American higher education during the three centuries of its development. There are excerpts from the charters and statutes of pioneer colonial institutions; from legislative acts, e.g., the Morrill Act; from reports of committees and commissions; and from the writings of leaders such as Francis Wayland, Andrew D. White, Daniel C. Gilman, William Rainey Harper and Charles W. Eliot. The final section of the book deals, perhaps inadequately, with twentieth-century issues and trends, with excerpts from the writings of Alexander Meiklejohn, John Dewey and Robert M. Hutchins. Nothing published since 1948 is included. While not for continuous, uninterrupted reading, the two volumes may well be kept at hand for frequent excursions into history, and, perhaps, escape from immediate pressures and renewal of devotion to one's larger purposes through communion with some of the "pioneering giants."

JACOB, PHILIP E., *Changing Values in College,* Harper and Brothers, New York, 1957, 174 + xvi pages

The subtitle characterizes the book as an "exploratory study of the impact of college teaching." It is in fact both less and more inclusive than this suggests. The central problem initially is stated as a study of "what changes do occur in students' patterns of value during college, and to what extent such changes stem from exposure to various types of *social science* in the 'general' part of the curriculum." Later, the study was extended "to include elements beyond the actual content and organization of courses—such as the impact of the instructor, of various methods of teaching, and of the 'climate' of particular institutions." A *Summary of Findings,* including a generalized "profile" of the values of the American college student, precedes the seven numbered chapters. These chapters digest and generalize from the findings of a wide variety of available studies; these sources are listed in the 36-page *Inventory of the Data* which concludes the book (pages 138-174). The "findings" are almost wholly negative. This fact challenges the reader to a critical reappraisal of his own assumptions as related to his own institution and to his own work. At the same time he is challenged to an equally critical appraisal of the assumptions and the methodology of the book itself.

MILLETT, JOHN D., *The Academic Community: An Essay on Organization,* McGraw-Hill Book Company, Inc., New York, 1962, 265 + ix pages

Will be most interesting and helpful to the college president concerned to relate practice to theory. A political scientist and one-time professor of public administration as well as a college president, the author devotes the initial chapter to a review of organizational theory as related to business and public administration, concluding with the suggestion that the usual concepts developed in these areas do not apply to colleges and universities, which are different "in institutional setting, in purpose, in operation, and hence in internal organization." Subsequent chapters elaborate the differences. "Instead of being organized upon the principles of a hierarchy of authority . . . colleges and universities are organized internally upon the principle of a community of authority," i.e., there is a "distribution of power" and the operation depends upon a consensus among four power groups: faculty, students, alumni, administration. A chapter is devoted to each of these four. The final chapter discusses the sources of conflict in the academic community and the factors making for consensus among the four power groups.

MOBBERLEY, DAVID G., and WICKE, MYRON F., *The Deanship of the Liberal Arts College,* Board of Education, The Methodist Church, Nashville, 1962, 72 pages

An introduction by a college president commends this "small volume as a valuable distillation of wisdom and experience." The three chapters deal with *The Dean and His Relationships, A Job Analysis* and *Some Selected Questions.* This is a much needed initial approach to a subject which invites more extensive and detailed analysis and exposition. It is to be hoped that the authors will find time to devote themselves to a more intensive and elaborate portrayal of the functions of this vitally important academic office.

RAUH, MORTON A., *College and University Trusteeship*, Antioch Press, Yellow Springs, Ohio, 1959, 112 pages

Based on interviews with trustees, presidents and faculty members, the book includes a number of illustrative case studies. A wide variety of views find expression. Of special interest to presidents will be Chapter 3 on *Board-President Relationships* and Chapter 7 on *Qualifications of Trustees*. Three appendices provide suggestions on trustee reading and reprint the statement of principles governing faculty relationships, as approved by the Association of American Colleges, the American Association of University Professors, and other organizations.

RUDOLPH, FREDERICK, *The American College and University; A History*, Alfred A. Knopf, Inc., New York, 1962, 516 pages

A competent account of the development of higher education in this country as an expression of the aspirations and ideals of the American people. There are analyses of curricular developments, changing patterns of financial support and control, and the burgeoning of extra-curricular activities, including athletics. While there may be omissions that will disappoint the reader, the book provides much that is helpful in interpreting current problems and trends. The chapters on *The Academic Balance of Power* and on *The Organized Institution* have special relevance to some of the president's administrative problems.

RUML, BEARDSLEY, and MORRISON, DONALD H., *Memo to a College Trustee*, McGraw-Hill Book Company, Inc., New York, 1959, 94 + viii pages

Presented as a Report on Financial and Structural Problems of the Liberal College and addressed to "a college trustee," this small volume is much more than a "report" and challenges the attention not alone of trustees but, perhaps even more directly, that of faculty and administrators of the colleges. It emphasizes the need for "internal improvements" and calls upon the trustees "as the locus of final responsibility and authority" to "take over" and play an informed and insistent part in effecting the improvements. There is sharply adverse criticism of much in current practice (curricular organization, academic calendars, schedules, class-size, methods of instruction). *The Models of the Possible* presents "a variety of patterns soundly designed to serve the economic requirements of an adequate scale of faculty compensation." There follows a discussion of alternative procedures and of the difficulties in effecting change, under the heading *The Achievement of the Possible*. The final chapter discusses *The Informed Trustee, a Major Responsibility of the President*. Responsible educators have seen both challenge and threat in the pronouncements of this publication.

SANFORD, NEVITT, Editor, *The American College—A Psychological and Social Interpretation of the Higher Learning*, John Wiley and Sons, Inc., New York, 1962, 1084 + xvi pages

The nature and purpose of this impressive, even formidable, book, are defined by the subtitle. "Modern social and personality theory" is applied to the study of higher education in a "searching, penetrating analysis by a group of outstanding social scientists." Thirty contributors; 28 chapters, most of which have a list of references at the end. The name index and the subject index together fill fifty pages. Typical chapter headings are: *The Viability of the American College; Personality and Interpersonal Relations in the College Classroom; The Curriculum in the Perspective of the Theory of Personality Development; Some Social-Psychological Theory for Selecting and Guiding College Students.* While admittedly dwelling "more upon the relatively unpalatable than upon that which calls for congratulations," the editor assures the reader that "this kind of socioanalysis, like psychoanalysis before it, is based on faith in the ultimate triumph of good sense." The book cannot be recommended to presidents for casual, spare-moments reading, nor for ready solutions to pressing practical problems. It may well be kept at hand for serious study when a busy president can take some extended "time off" for checking his experience and his own commitments against this systematic, scientific charting of "the way into relatively unexplored territory."

SCHMIDT, GEORGE P., *The Liberal Arts College; A Chapter in American Cultural History*, Rutgers University Press, New Brunswick, New Jersey, 1957, 310 + viii pages

A lively and readable "chronicle of the liberal arts college as an element in American cultural history." The story is vitalized by the treatment of developments and controversies in terms of personalities rather than as abstractions. "Students, professors, presidents, trustees, and alumni, appear as persons and not categories." Chapter Nine, *Transformation and Rival Loyalties,* provides trenchant commentary on intercollegiate athletics and on fraternities. The final three chapters deal with twentieth-century issues and trends: *Dewey vs. Hutchins; The Liberal Arts College Today,* and *Academic Freedom.* There are 32 pages of notes, arranged by chapters. A *Bibliographical Note* follows.

SINGLETON, GORDON G., and others, *The College or University Dean,* Baylor University Press, Waco, Texas, 1955, 47 pages

Report of a pioneer study conducted by a graduate class in education. Seven brief chapters deal with the qualifications and the relationships of the dean. The longest and perhaps the most insightful and helpful chapter is that dealing with *The Dean and Instruction.*

STOKE, HAROLD W., *The American College President,* Harper and Brothers, New York, 1959, 180 pages

"This book is not a guide to the would-be college president, nor a handbook on how to administer the office. It is meant, rather, as an interpretation of an important part of higher education, a report on some of the problems of the president, and an indication of some of the pleasures and pains of his position." The writing is marked by such extraordinary clarity and grace as to make it delightful reading. But the penetrating insight, the candor and the understanding wisdom make it equally rewarding. Memorable paragraphs are found in each of the ten chapters. On almost any of his immediate concerns a president will find pointed and helpful comment. Unusual are the pages in Chapter I (*The Vested Authority*) on the choice of a president; in Chapter II on *The President's Personal Problems;* Chapter VII on *The President Among Scholars;* and Chapter IX on *The Uneasy Campus.*

TICKTON, SIDNEY G., *Needed: A Ten Year College Budget,* Fund for the Advancement of Education, New York, 1961, 40 pages

A compact (16 pages) presentation of conditions demanding of the colleges careful advance planning and of "hot" questions that must be faced is followed by a College Case Study (reprinted from an earlier publication) and by a packet of nine worksheets for use in projecting budgets for the ten years 1962-1971. Such projections may well be—may have been—for many a president a "soul searching exercise." There is need, however, for insistent emphasis on the point that such a projection should not "be looked upon as a fixed, unchangeable blueprint"; that such long-range planning is a continuing job, with recognition of the need for revision and readjustment "in the light of the social and economic changes occurring on the campus and in the country at large."

TRUEBLOOD, D. ELTON, *The Idea of A College,* Harper and Brothers, New York, 1959, 207 + x pages

By the widely known author, lecturer and professor of philosophy who "chose a small college," this book will bring inspiration and challenge to any president who shares the devotion to the liberal arts college, especially the Christian college, which motivates the writing throughout. After two chapters which orient the reader to the point of view, there follow, among others, chapters on *The Teacher, The Student, Administration, Curriculum,* and *The College As A Community.* The final two chapters discuss *Integrity* and *The Vision of Excellence.* In no sense a "how to" book, it nevertheless touches on many practical aspects of present-day college administration. The discussions are marked by an enviable assurance and by a combination of idealism and realistic common sense.

WICKE, MYRON F., *Handbook for Trustees,* Board of Education, The Methodist Church, Nashville, Revised Edition, 1962, 101 pages

Concise practical discussions of the responsibilities and the relationships of governing boards. Seven chapters, the last of which is *A Note to Trustees of Church-Related Colleges.* The revised edition incorporates new material, including a reading list and three appendices on *Academic*

*Freedom and Tenure, Faculty Participation in College and University Government,* and *Procedural Standards in Faculty Dismissal Procedures.* With some commentary, these present the familiar statements of principles approved by influential educational bodies.

WOODBURNE, LLOYD S., *Principles of College and University Administration,* Stanford University Press, Stanford, California, 1958, 197 pages

The twelve chapters deal with guiding principles in most of the areas of administrative decision making. The analyses of organization and procedures are admirably straightforward and practical, though no rigid prescriptions are made. "There is no one correct solution to each administrative problem in higher education." Thus, on the basis of the stated principles a "choice for the reader" is provided to fit the conditions and the needs of his own institution. Unusual separate chapters are devoted to *Departmental Administration* and to *Nonacademic Personnel.* The bibliography lists chronologically publications on general administration appearing between 1908 and 1953.

WRISTON, HENRY M., *Academic Procession; Reflections of a College President,* Columbia University Press, New York, 1959, 222 pages

An "intensely personal book, consisting of reflections upon experiences of more than thirty years." The author insists that it "makes no pretense to supply a guide. There is no mold in which college presidents can be shaped—and called good. Each must do what he does in his own way." With no punches pulled, the writing is marked by complete and sometimes startling candor. It is good reading. Many a college president will find himself keeping it close at hand for repeated rereading. There are chapters on *The Trustees, The Faculty, The Administration, The Students, The Alumni* and *The Public.*

# Index